For

I first met Greg when we purchased a house next to his in East Helena, Montana. As we were unloading our U-Haul he came over and introduced himself and like new neighbors do, we got to know each other over the next few months. He said he was a preacher and I wondered what that was since I'd been raised in a pretty traditional religion; and he didn't look like what I expected from a religious leader. He was a pretty normal guy.

He saw that I had a bird dog and asked if I'd take him pheasant hunting which I gladly did a few months later. As we drove, I asked him if he was like a priest or something and his reply was, "No I'm just one beggar telling other beggars where to find bread. I share the message of Jesus and eternal life with those who want to hear it." I thought that was interesting then our conversation changed to birds, dogs and hunting in Montana.

We shot some birds (Greg missed a lot) then on the way home he said he had a series of Bible studies that helped people understand how to build their relationship with God and the first one started with what the Bible claimed about Jesus. He asked if I'd like to look at the first lesson to see if I'd be interested in looking at the others. I was resistant and told him to just give me the study and I'd look at it and get back with him. Of course; I never did.

A couple months later Greg and I were talking and he asked me if I'd ever looked at the study he'd given me; which I hadn't. He then offered, "Why don't you invite me over and we'll go over the first study to see if it's something that you're interested in? I promise I'll never try to talk you into anything, but I think you'll enjoy it. When can we get together?" I reluctantly agreed and told him that I didn't want someone trying to sell me some religion. "If we begin this study and I decide it is not for me and I say 'I'm done;' then I'm done." He agreed.

Greg came over and we sat at our dinner table and he gave me a Bible and had me open to the table of contents and explained how it was organized. He then gave me the study guide and walked me through the first study "Who is Jesus." When we finished, I was amazed and said that

I'd learned more in one hour about Jesus and the Bible than I'd learned my entire life. I asked Greg if he'd come back and go through this study with my wife, Ade. Of course he agreed. I guess I didn't expect Ade's initial reluctance though. She wanted no part of it!

We set a time for Ade to get off work and join us. She purposely delayed more than an hour coming home because she assumed she'd be exposed to some religious "high pressure" presentation where she'd be forced into something she had no interest in. Her eyes rolled when she walked in; but when she joined us, Greg went through the study as he did with me and she experienced the same thing I did. She wanted to learn more. Both of us agreed that we'd learned more about the Bible and Jesus in the first hour with Greg than we'd learned our entire life.

We examined our life and relationship with God as a result of these studies and our lives have not been the same since. We started a small group Bible study at our home and invited all our friends to listen to the Good News we'd learned. Many of our friends and family have been through these studies and many lives have been changed. It is unlike anything I could have ever imagined!

If you're a religious person; you need to read this book. Your faith will be strengthened. If you're an atheist; take a look and open your mind to things you may not have considered. If you're on the fence; take a look and honestly see what this book can teach you. Ade's dad Joe was a hardnosed stubborn guy. He met Greg and also reluctantly agreed to look at these studies over coffee. Greg and he became close friends and Joe became a believer in Christ from what he learned. He died a few years ago and I believe he has eternal life from what he learned going through these easy-to-understand studies on how to build your relationship with God.

Little did I know that meeting Greg and listening to these lessons would have such a profound impact on my life; my family; and the multitude of people I've met because of allowing my neighbor to share bread with another beggar. I'm glad I did, and I hope you are too, as you read this book.

Shaun Peterson

Introduction

I saw an interview with a one hundred and eight year old lady in Fargo, ND recently. She said she really didn't feel any older than she did when she was a hundred; and everyone laughed. I'm sure you'll agree that one hundred eight years old is a long time to live. But I want you to think about this; when you stop living in your present body, you're going to step out into eternity. How will you feel a thousand years – or one hundred thousand years from now? Eternity never ends. You'll be alive one billion years from now. So the question is, where will you be? Once you step into eternity, your fate is sealed, not for a hundred years, but for trillions of years. If you're like most of the human race, you think about this from time to time, and you think about it more the older you get. The Bible says, "God has set eternity in the hearts of men," (Ecclesiastes 3:11). This is a book to help you seriously consider and prepare for eternity. It is the most important decision you'll ever consider.

Men have started religions to try to get in touch with God because we all think about eternity. But did you know that God is not interested in religion? Now that's an unusual statement to open a book with. May-be you believe there is a God or a Higher Power but you're not interested in religion either. Good, because I want you to open your mind to the idea of a relationship and not religion. There are a lot of religions in the world and a lot of bad stuff has happened in the name of religion as I'm sure you're aware. Is there a difference between Buddha, Mohammed, and Jesus? If so, what's the big deal anyway? Can I be saved and go to heaven with either, or is it necessary to even discuss the issue? Can't I just be a good enough person and ignore this whole discussion? No, you really can't and I hope you will read on with an open mind to see what's about to happen to you when you step into eternity. It's a big deal!

I had lunch with a PhD scientist in Canada a few years back. As we sat over lunch in Vancouver, British Columbia, he told me he didn't believe in God (in the sense of religion) but he did believe logically that there had to be a supreme energy in the universe that was also supreme intelligence. He called that energy "CHI" (chee). He told me that after considering the complexity of the universe and a DNA molecule, he was forced logically to conclude that there had to be some supreme intelligence and energy that started the universe and created life. It was just too complex and well-designed for it to just happen by chance.

Think about it this way. Do you think that a highly advanced computer program could first make the computer then write itself? That would be ridiculous, right? Bill Gates, in *The Road Ahead,* said "DNA is like a computer program but far, far more advanced than any software ever created." The genetic code written into a single DNA molecule staggers the imagination of the most intelligent scientific minds of our time. If the code was strung out line by line it would actually go to moon and back multiple times. And each living things' DNA molecule is individually written and coded with no duplicates! It programs your seven trillion cells with extremely precise intelligent instructions. Even the Krebs Cycle inside of the cell and its internal communication system that instructs the cell when to repair or replace itself is all programmed into a single DNA molecule that even replicates itself. The DNA genetic code instructs this cell to become a heart cell, and another to become an eye, and yet another to be a brain cell. You think that can be an accident of evolution or random chance? I don't have that much faith! Any logical, intelligent and well-informed person must admit that there has to be a Creator, or supreme intelligence that wrote the program for life for each individual and the universe. My friend called that CHI. Plato called it *Logos.* Most people acknowledge that Supreme power and Intelligence as God.

I asked my scientist friend if he was aware that the Bible actually claimed that CHI, the Supreme Intelligence of the universe, became a man and lived among us for a while. He jumped to his feet and hit the table and exclaimed, "Why has no one ever told me THAT before? I want to hear more about this!" You'll learn about this concept as you read through the book. You may jump up and hit the table as well!

This book is designed to give you simple, easy-to-understand information so that you can be better prepared to make your own *informed* decisions. We'll examine the most ancient spiritual manuscript in human history – the Bible. More copies of the Bible have been purchased than any other piece of literature in the world and yet many know very little about it. You'll learn a little about its history in the beginning of the book. If you want to hear the most documented and ancient information about eternal life and the spiritual world then you will want to listen closely.

Much of the information you will learn in this book is not taught in most places. Some of it may offend you and that's OK because sometimes the cage around the zoo needs to be kicked. There's nothing in this book that is sugar-coated. My intent is to show you some of the absurd statements of the Bible and the outlandish claims that it makes about Jesus. After seeing them, you'll either hate Him as did the Jews and Romans of the first century, or you'll open your eyes to things you never before considered. He's called *"A stone of stumbling and rock of offense"* for a reason. I hope you aren't offended and don't stumble at what you're about to read, but if you do you're not alone. Billions over the centuries have sadly been offended.

If you already follow Jesus, you may also be offended by some of the things in this book. As I said, much of what is in here is not being taught so be forewarned. Your beliefs will be challenged. You won't find opinions here. You'll see multitudes of Jesus' followers turn away offended after hearing what He told them. After the crowds left, He even turned to His own apostles and asked them if they wanted to leave also! They answered, "Lord, to whom shall we go, you have words of eternal life!" Jesus is very confrontational, and not the white-robed timid guy you might be used to hearing about in church. These are things you aren't being told in church if you attend! I'll show you actual documentation and let you read it for yourself. No "touchy-feely" politically correct information will be shared here. Your eternity is too important for speculation and subjective interpretation.

Let me invite you to join me and explore the real truth about Your Relationship with God. You're smart enough to see if what you're reading is opinion or fact. Buckle down and enjoy the read. I'm trying to write this just as if I were sitting across your kitchen table with a cup of coffee and letting you read this information for yourself.

I'm just one beggar telling other beggars where to find free bread. This bread I'm telling you about is the Bread of Life – Eternal Life. Eat till you're full! My intent is that you find the truth that gives you grace, peace and assurance for eternal life! Get your pride out of the way and listen to what God is trying to tell you. He loves you deeply and unconditionally and sometimes the truth hurts, but be assured that He is madly in love with you."For God so loved the world that He gave His only begotten Son, that whoever believes in him should not perish, but have eternal life," (John 3:16). I pray for you that your heart will listen. "He who has ears to hear, let him hear!" Are you listening?

Greg King

Contents

Chapter 1 - How to Understand Your Bible

 The Bible is the number one selling piece of literature purchased throughout the world! A*nnual* Bible sales in America alone are worth between $425 million and $650 million. Gideon International gives away a Bible every second. The Bible is available all or in part in 2,426 languages, covering 95% of the world's population. According to Guinness World Records, the Bible is the best-selling book of all time with over 5 billion copies sold and distributed. [1] That's a pretty big accomplishment and it's been that way for centuries! To put that in perspective, 5 Billion is huge when compared to the next rivals – Harry Potter Series – 450 million, The Lord of the Rings – 150 million, The Hobbit- 140.6 million and so on. [2] Compare the Bible with any and every book ever written and you'll quickly see that *it is the most popular and magnificent piece of literature in human history.*

Let that statement sink in for a minute. The Bible is the #1 most significant piece of literature in **ALL** of human history! People have been imprisoned and even died to read the Bible or even acquire a copy of it. Cultures have changed because of it. It alone has been the motivation for hospitals, orphanages, elimination of slavery and human rights movements around the world. In America we have free access to the Bible and many homes have multiple copies in a variety of translations. You can even download a free Bible app (www.bible.com) with multiple translations and languages. Don't let its easy availability cause you to miss its splendor.

---

[1] http://www.guinnessworldrecords.com/world-records/best-selling-book-of-non-fiction

[2] https://en.wikipedia.org/wiki/List_of_best-selling_books

When you hold a Bible in your hand you need to appreciate that <u>you are touching the most sought after piece of literature in the history of the world!</u> People in countries like China are willing to jeopardize their freedom just to obtain a copy of a book that many of us take for granted, and many know very little about. I hope you learn in our time together how to navigate, read, and understand the Bible you have in your hands! It's the only book that documents the origin of the world, the human race, how different languages originated, and the history of the Middle East and specifically the beginning of the nation of Israel. When you watch CNN and the news about what's happening in the Middle East, it all started in the book of Genesis.

There are "Translations" and there are "Paraphrases" of the Bible. A paraphrase is when the text is given a present day "paraphrase" of what the text *sorta* says. Paraphrases can be OK if you want a general feel of a text. Paraphrases should not be relied upon if you're seeking for what the actual text said in the original language. You should use a translation in that case.

Translations are when a group of scholars work together in a very lengthy, strenuous and tedious manner to take the original text (Hebrew, Aramaic or Greek) and translate it as accurately as possible into a particular language, whether it is English, Spanish or other present day languages. My wife speaks Romanian as her native tongue, and English as her second. She also understands Italian, Spanish, and a bit of French and Arabic. Even though she was taught English as a girl in Romania and has been speaking it for decades, she still continues to confuse idioms, adverbs, adjectives and sentence structure. For instance, when she wants me to buy soap for our dish washer, she'll often say, "Honey, please get me some "soap dish." Her Romanian mind puts it in a different structure than English. A Frenchman might want to order Blue Cheese on his salad. In French its *fromage du bleu* – literally "cheese the blue." If we translated it from French to English literally, it sounds awkward and doesn't match English rules.

English is a fluid language and word meanings and idioms change over time, often quite rapidly. Even among English speaking countries, words mean different things. For instance, in Canada, a lady in her 70s or 80s might ask if you'd like a *"serviette"* with your coffee and invite you to join her on the *"chesterfield"* or "d*avenport."* She just asked you if you'd like a napkin and would you join her on the couch. Idioms from the 60s like *"groovy"* or *"far out"* meant, "Nifty, fantastic, excellent" and were later replaced by another generation to *"Rad!"* If you translated *"groovy"* literally, it would mean "something with grooves in it – like a weathered board." *"Far Out"* would mean something at a long distance. So when translators struggle to put the *meaning* of a word or phrase into another language so that the reader accurately understands what is being said it can present a challenge.

For instance, the King's James Bible was translated in 1611 for Classical English speaking audiences. Those were the same people who read Shakespeare and spoke like that in their daily lives. That form of English was the common language of the day used in commerce and poetry. When a person would read the King's James Bible they spoke in their daily conversation with terms like "Thou" and "Thee" and "Superfluity of Naughtiness". Today, we say "You" and say "The evil that is so prevalent."

Each "Translation" has an intended audience and that's why you'll see a variety of different translations available to you. Are the translators addressing academics or are they addressing the common person on the street in terms that can both be accurate and understandable? The American Standard Version is considered one of the most *literal* English translations, and it can be a bit choppy and awkward as you read it but even it has to make the structure of the original fit into an English structure. The English Standard Version on the other hand, is easier to read and its translating scholars had as their goal an accurate, yet more understandable format of the word structures for an English audience.

For the purpose of our time together, I recommend a few easy-to-use English Translations that are both accurate to the text and at the same time understandable to the common person. They are the New International Version, the New Kings James Version, and The New American Standard Version. I'll be quoting from these versions and recommend that you keep this study simple and have confidence in these three translations. Remember this - NO other piece of literature in human history has been more scrutinized and cross referenced and analyzed by higher textual critics than the Bible. You can be assured you have an accurate translation of the most important pieces of literature in human history in your hands with one of these translations.

How are the Books of the Bible Organized?

There are 66 books in the Bible that comprise a library. Look at the table of contents below. There you will find two major divisions: The Old Testament, and the New Testament. There are 39 books in the Old Testament, and 27 in the New Testament. The books are organized into sections like a mini library. To see a video explanation of this visit my site - (www.gregbiblestudy.blogspot.com).

66 Books – 40 Writers – 1,500 Years to Write – 4,000 Years of History			
OLD TESTAMENT		**NEW TESTAMENT**	
LAW	**POETRY**	**GOSPELS**	
GENESIS	JOB	MATTHEW	LUKE
EXODUS	PSALMS	MARK	JOHN
LEVITICUS	PROVERBS	**HISTORY**	
NUMBERS	ECCLESIASTES	ACTS OF THE APOSTLES	
DEUTERONOMY	SONG OF SOLOMON		
HISTORY	**MAJOR PROPHETS**	**PAUL'S LETTERS**	**GENERAL LETTERS**
JOSHUA	ISAIAH	ROMANS	JAMES
JUDGES	JEREMIAH	1 CORINTHIANS	1 PETER
RUTH	LAMENTATIONS	2 CORINTHIANS	2 PETER
1 SAMUEL	EZEKIEL	GALATIANS	1 JOHN
2 SAMUEL	DANIEL	EPHESIANS	2 JOHN
1 KINGS	**MINOR PROPHETS**	PHILIPPIANS	3 JOHN
2 KINGS	HOSEA	NAHUM	COLOSSIANS	JUDE
1 CHRONICLES	JOEL	HABAKKUK	1 THESSALONIANS	
2 CHRONICLES	AMOS	ZEPHANIAH	2 THESSALONIANS	**PROPHECY**
EZRA	OBADIAH	HAGGAI	1 TIMOTHY	REVELATION
NEHEMIAH	JONAH	ZECHARIAH	2 TIMOTHY	
ESTHER	MICAH	MALACHI	TITUS	
			PHILEMON	
			HEBREWS	

This is how the books of the Bible are organized. Remember, the Bible is a library of 66 books, categorized into sections. There are two major sections- Old Testament and New Testament. The Old Testament is divided into 5 sections. Law of Moses – 5 books. Jewish History – 12 books. Poetry – 5 books. Major Prophets – 5 books. Minor Prophets – 12 books. The New Testament is divided into 5 sections- Gospels- 4 books, History- 1 book, Paul's Letters- 14 books, General Letters- 7 books, Prophecy- 1 book.

In the original text there were no chapter and verse divisions. These were added later to help people navigate to a particular section of text. For instance, "Luke" is the book... 3:13... chapter 3 and verse 13. If it were John 1:1-14, it would be the Gospel of John, chapter 1 verses 1 through 14. I hope this helps as you begin your personal study. In this book I'll quote the verses so you won't have to look them up, but please feel free to do so and get to know your Bible personally.

Now let's have some fun as together we explore *Building Your Relationship with God.* Grab your Bible and let's see what it claims about Jesus. Note, you can also see a video of me presenting this lesson by clicking the Bible picture at www.gregbiblestudy.blogspot.com.

God bless as you begin Building Your Relationship with God!

Chapter 2 - Who is Jesus?

Have you really ever considered the incredible claims that the Bible makes about this man - Jesus of Nazareth? What makes Him different from Buddha or Mohammed? Is He different or is He just one of many "good" religious men in history? A lot of people claim a lot of things about themselves and about others. If you want to really grasp the impact of the Christian claim, then you have to sit back and comprehend the full force of what is claimed about Jesus in the Bible.

I want you to imagine you've never heard about Jesus and listen carefully to the statements about Him. If you hear them for the first time, you have to logically conclude that Jesus and His followers are making some outlandish claims. It will help you understand why people hated Him and ultimately killed Him because of His claims. People don't kill nice guys who are just a little bit controversial or insane. Jesus made some claims about Himself that were so divisive and, in the minds of His hearers, heretical, that they killed Him in a public and horrible way. Why did they react in this way? What claims can a man make that cause Him to be so hated?

In this chapter you will discover what the Bible **claims** about this man so that you will be better prepared to make an objective decision of whether or not to be one of His followers.

I. Jesus was an actual historical figure

Luke 3:1-2; 21

In the fifteenth year of the reign of Tiberius Caesar—when Pontius Pilate was governor of Judea, Herod tetrarch of Galilee, his brother Philip tetrarch of Iturea and Traconitis, and Lysanias tetrarch of Abilene— during the high-priesthood of Annas and

Caiaphas, the word of God came to John son of Zechariah in the wilderness

When all the people were being baptized, Jesus was baptized too. And as he was praying, heaven was opened.

There are at least twelve non-Christian sources that mention Jesus and his crucifixion. Sources like Josephus, a Jewish historian of the first century. A "tetrarch" was a ruler or magistrate over a region. Jesus is placed in an actual historical setting with Roman officials like Herod, Pilate and Caesar. If you were to research ancient Roman history, you would find these men listed.

It's important to know that regardless of people's beliefs about Jesus' claims, no one can deny that He was an actual historical figure.

II. Jesus existed in the beginning

John 1:1-2; 14-18

In the beginning was the Word, and the Word was with God, and the Word was God. He was with God in the beginning...The Word became flesh and made his dwelling among us. We have seen His glory, the glory of the one and only Son, who came from the Father, full of grace and truth.

John testified concerning Him. He cried out, saying, "This is the one I spoke about when I said, 'He who comes after me has surpassed me because he was before me." Out of his fullness we have all received grace in place of grace already given. For the law was given through Moses; grace and truth came through Jesus Christ. No one has ever seen God, but the one and only Son, who is Himself God and is in closest relationship with the Father, has made Him known.

John is thought to have been quoting Plato in the first few verses of his Gospel. The term *Word (Logos in Greek)* should not be understood to mean that the *written word* became flesh. The idea of *Logos* in Plato's mind is that of the Supreme Idea or Divine Reason of the universe.

If you were to ask Plato, "Where was this table before it was made?" Plato's response would be, "It was in the MIND of the one who made it, because before anything can come into being, it must first be an idea or reason in the mind." If you were to ask Plato, "Where was the universe before it came into being?" Plato's response would be something like, "It was made from Divine Reason or the Supreme Idea which he termed *Logos.*" So, when you read John's words *"In the beginning was the Word (Logos – Divine Reason – Supreme Idea)* you must understand that he is talking about the Divine Reason of the universe – God.

What Plato never conceived is verse 14, "The Word (*Logos – Divine Reason – Supreme Idea)* became flesh!

> *"That there is a Divine Reason in the universe, and that this universal Logos is none other than He who is life and light of men and who in the fullness of time became flesh."* [3]

These verses make some outlandish claims here about Jesus of Nazareth.
- It acknowledges that the Word (Logos – The Supreme Idea) was in the beginning and the source of creation.
- Then it claims that the Logos became flesh (a man) and lived for a while among us – namely, Jesus. That's a pretty wild claim, don't you think?

> *John 8:56-59*
>
> *Your father Abraham rejoiced at the thought of seeing my day; he saw it and was glad." "You are not yet fifty years old," they said to Him, "and you have seen Abraham!" "Very truly I tell you, "Jesus answered, "Before Abraham was born, I am!" At this, they picked up stones to stone Him, but Jesus hid Himself, slipping away from the temple grounds.*

When Jesus made this statement, Abraham had been dead for over 1,000 years already. Did Jesus claim that He was before Abraham? Absolutely! There is no other religious leader who claims to have

---

[3](http://www.ccel.org/ccel/orr/view.xxii.vi.ii.html?highlight=plato,word,became,flesh #highlight).

existed from before the beginning of time and the creation – at least none that are sane!

Now understand the impact of Jesus claiming this. Option 1- He lied and knew He was lying. Option 2 – He was a lunatic and speaking as a crazy man who thought He was God. Option 3 – He claimed to be from before the beginning of time and it was true!

But don't forget this. Jesus believed He was God and those who killed Him understood clearly that is what He believed and that was their reason for murdering Him. They didn't kill Him because he was a nice guy preaching love your enemy and forgive everybody! They killed Him on grounds of blaspheme because He claimed to be the God of the Universe in human flesh!

> *Liar, Lunatic or Lord?*
> *You must decide!*

III. Jesus is the God of the universe who became flesh

John 1:1, 14

In the beginning was the Word, and the Word was with God, and the Word was God. And the Word was made flesh, and dwelt among us, (and we beheld his glory, the glory as of the only begotten of the Father,) full of grace and truth.

In these verses, again we see clearly demonstrated that the Word (Logos) was in the beginning and was God. And in verse 14 the Word (God, Logos - the Supreme Idea of the universe) became flesh.

> *The Jews tried desperately to kill Him; not because He was loving little children, or even healing people. They understood that He claimed to be God and that deserved death.*

I hope you listening to these claims as though you were hearing them for the first time. The Bible is claiming that Jesus of Nazareth is the God of the universe who became flesh! That's either ridiculous, or amazing, depending upon its validity. It's either true or false!

9

John 5:18

For this reason they tried all the more to kill Him; not only was he breaking the Sabbath, but he was even calling God his own Father, making Himself equal with God.

The Jews tried desperately to kill Him; not because He was loving little children, or even healing people. They understood that He claimed to be God! The penalty for blaspheme was to be stoned. I think it's amazing as you read through the New Testament to see the religious leaders' reaction to Jesus. They killed Him because He claimed to be God yet wasn't religious enough for them and He hung around the wrong kind of people – sinners!

John 10:30-33

I and the Father are one." Again His Jewish opponents picked up stones to stone Him, but Jesus said to them, "I have shown you many good works from the Father. For which of these do you stone me?" "We are not stoning you for any good work," they replied, "but for blasphemy, because <u>you, a mere man, claim to be God</u>."

Now here's a very interesting verse found in the book of Hebrews. It's showing that Jesus is superior to the angels.

Hebrews 1:4-8

So he became as much superior to the angels as the name he has inherited is superior to theirs. For to which of the angels did God ever say, "You are my Son; Today I have become your Father"? Or again, "I will be his Father, and he will be my Son"?

And again, when God brings his firstborn into the world, he says, "Let all God's angels worship Him."

In speaking of the angels he says, "He makes his angels spirits, and his servants flames of fire."

But about the Son he says, "Your throne, O God, will last forever and ever; a scepter of justice will be the scepter of your kingdom.

Let's take a closer look at this passage. The author is demonstrating Jesus' superiority over angels by asking some rhetorical questions.

"To which of the angels did God ever say "You are my Son"?

Well, God never did call an angel His Son and never claimed to be a Father to any angels. However when God brought Jesus into the world He says, *"Let all God's angels worship Him."* We have record of the angels worshipping in Luke 2:13, *"And suddenly there was a great multitude of heavenly hosts praising God and saying, 'Glory to God in the highest, and on earth peace among men in whom he is well pleased!"*

> The crowd is discussing whether or not this crazy man is the one the Jewish leaders were trying to kill.

Think about this. The first of the Ten Commandments is, *"I am the Lord your God… you shall have no other gods before me, you shall not bow down to them or worship them for I, the Lord am your God!" (Exodus 20:1-5).* So if God commands angels to worship Jesus, and He says that no other god is to be worshipped, that means that Jesus is legitimately God or else the angels were worshipping a false god and would be guilty of idolatry.

In verse 8 notice what God says about His son Jesus, *"But your throne, **O God**, will last forever and ever"*. Here we have God, the Father, calling Jesus God. The Bible describes God in three persons, Father, Son, and Holy Spirit, and yet still only One God.

IV. Jesus is the only one who knows God

> *Matthew 11:27*
> *"All things have been committed to me by my Father. No one knows the Son except the Father, and no one knows the Father except the Son and those to whom the Son chooses to reveal Him.*

In this verse, Jesus said that "No one knows the Son, except the Father, and no one knows the Father except the Son *and* those to whom the Son chooses to reveal Him." Let's see why Jesus made this statement.

> *John 7:25-29*
>
> *At that point some of the people of Jerusalem began to ask, "Isn't this the man they are trying to kill? Here he is, speaking publicly, and they are not saying a word to Him. Have the authorities really concluded that he is the Messiah? But we know where this man is from; when the Messiah comes, no one will know where he is from."*
>
> *Then Jesus, still teaching in the temple courts, cried out, "Yes, you know me, and you know where I am from. I am not here on my own authority, but he who sent me is true. You do not know Him, but I know Him because I am from Him and He sent me."*

I have to keep reminding myself that I'm looking back in time to these historical events. If I was one of the people in the crowd, I wonder if I would have been as skeptical as some of those people.

The crowd is discussing whether or not this crazy man is the one the Jewish leaders were trying to kill. He was speaking publicly, yet no one was saying a word, and they began making foolish statements. *"We know this guy and where he's from."* They thought he was from Nazareth and in another place said, *"Can any good thing come from Nazareth?" (John 1:46).* He was actually born in Bethlehem, but that's not really where He is from. He claims to be from heaven.

He said He was from God His Father and He sent Him. Remember our discussion above about Plato and his concept of Logos – the Supreme Idea? The philosophers also had the concept of a two story universe, the spiritual and the physical, or that which is *above* (the spiritual) and that which is *below* (the physical). The spiritual realm they referred to as *pleroma (play-roma).*

John's Gospel is written to an audience influenced by Greek Philosophy. Some refer to this as Metaphysical Theism: God Exists in the Pleroma, the World of 'Forms'. Plato taught that the universe was caused by God, who is *"Pure Mind"*, or the Supreme Idea. It was Plato's idea that God exists in the Pleroma, which he believed to be the *only* reality. The Pleroma, he taught, lies above and outside the unreal, illusory or "phenomenal" universe in which men exist (the physical or the realm of *below*). It was believed that God exists outside of time and space and really had little interest in that which was below.

> **When one who understood Plato's concept of the universe heard these claims of Jesus, it would have been a jaw-dropping claim! I hope you feel the same.**

The objective of Philosophy (a compound word meaning *Wisdom Lovers*) was to achieve a level of enlightenment and knowledge of truth by which they could tap into the Pleroma and thus attain a certain spiritual awakening placing themselves in contact with the mind of God. They never in their wildest imagination would ever conceive that the Logos – Pure Mind, Truth, and The Supreme Idea of the Universe would ever bother to connect with the lower realm of that which is below. Jesus is about to blow their minds with the following claims.

John 8:23

"But he continued, "You are from below; I am from above. You are of this world; I am not of this world"

John 16:28

"I came from the Father and entered the world; now I am leaving the world and going back to the Father."

Did you catch it? Jesus said, "You are from below, I'm from above." I am from *Pleroma*, the spiritual realm; you are of this world – the realm of below. I came from the spiritual world and entered the world, and I'm leaving and going back!

13

Jesus claims that He knew God, because He was from God and God sent Him into the realm of *below*. When one who understood Plato's concept of the universe heard these claims of Jesus, it would have been a jaw-dropping claim! I hope you feel the same.

V. Jesus came to reveal the Father to mankind

As I already mentioned, the objective of the Greek Philosopher was to know *truth* and to be enlightened. Enlightenment and the pursuit of real knowledge and real truth was the *Way* to tap into the Pleroma. To know truth was to have light and life. Jesus dashes their aspirations when He said, *"I am the way, and the truth and the life. No man comes to the Father except by me" (John 14:6).*

Jesus' purpose in coming was to give man truth and real life and to know God – the Pure Mind, the Supreme Idea of the Universe. By *knowledge of God* they could achieve life that is life indeed – eternal life! Having now some background in Greek thought wrap your mind around what John writes in the following verses that we've already introduced above. It is not man's effort to achieve enlightenment, but God, the Logos, becoming flesh in the person of Jesus that made God known to those in the realm below – those in darkness.

> *John 1:1-5; 14-18*
>
> *In the beginning was the Word, and the Word was with God, and the Word was God. He was with God in the beginning. Through Him all things were made; without Him nothing was made that has been made. In Him was life, and that life was the light of all mankind. The light shines in the darkness, and the darkness did not comprehend it.*
>
> *The true light, which gives light to everyone, was coming into the world. He was in the world, and the world was made through Him, yet the world did not know Him. He came to his own, and his own did not receive Him. But to all who did receive Him, who believed in his name, he gave the right to become children of*

God, who were born, not of blood nor of the will of the flesh nor of the will of man, but of God.

And the Word became flesh and dwelt among us, and we have seen his glory, glory as of the only Son from the Father, full of grace and truth. (John bore witness about Him, and cried out, "This was he of whom I said, 'He who comes after me ranks before me, because he was before me.'"). For from his fullness we have all received, grace upon grace. For the law was given through Moses; grace and truth came through Jesus Christ. No one has ever seen God; the only God, who is at the Father's side, he has made Him known.

Wow! This has to be one of the most powerful declarations in all of human history! In the beginning was the Word – Logos, the Pure Mind or Supreme Idea of the universe. He is the creator of everything that has been made and is Himself the light and that which gives life to men who are in darkness and can't comprehend or wrap their minds around what God is doing.

The true light, not the attempt at enlightenment of the philosopher, came into this world and those who receive Him not only receive life, but are born of God and become His children. The Word, the Logos, became flesh and literally, *pitched his tent here for a while.* No one has ever seen God or known Him in spite of their desperate pursuit of knowledge and enlightenment. However, God, the Word, became flesh to make Himself known to those below! Jesus and He alone made God known. Pretty amazing claim huh?

Hebrews 1:1-3

In the past God spoke to our ancestors through the prophets at many times and in various ways, but in these last days he has spoken to us by his Son, whom he appointed heir of all things, and through whom also he made the universe. The Son is the radiance of God's glory and the exact representation of his being, sustaining all things by his powerful word. After he had provided purification for sins, he sat down at the right hand of the Majesty in heaven.

God in the Old Testament times spoke to men like Abraham, Isaac, Jacob, Elijah and Moses in a variety of ways and at different times. But now He speaks to us by His Son (the Logos who became flesh) who is also the one who made the universe.

The Son – Jesus – is the radiance of God's glory, and the exact representation of His being and nature and the one who sustains and holds the universe together. He came to provide purification for our sins by his death on the cross, then ascended back to the Pleroma – back to the spiritual realm and sat down on the throne of David as ruler over the universe as King of kings and Lord of lords!

> **If you've seen Jesus, you've seen the God of the universe in human flesh and His purpose was to make God known – to give light to those in darkness – to know the truth and to allow men to be born of God and receive eternal life.**

John 14:6-9

Jesus answered, "I am the way and the truth and the life. No one comes to the Father except through me. If you really know me, you will know my Father as well. From now on, you do know Him and have seen Him." Philip said, "Lord, show us the Father and that will be enough for us." Jesus answered: "Don't you know me, Philip, even after I have been among you such a long time? Anyone who has seen me has seen the Father. How can you say, 'Show us the Father'?

Jesus came to make God known to those in darkness, those in the lower realm, and those in the flesh. In order to do this, He Himself became flesh. Here's another one of those *jaw-dropping* encounters in the Bible. Jesus is telling His disciples that if they really knew Him, they would know God and from now on they do know Him and have *seen* Him. Phillip, just like us, didn't quite catch the drift of what Jesus just said, so he comes up with a great idea! "Jesus, just show us God. Open the sky and let us peak at Him!" Jesus replied, "Don't you know me Philip; even after I have been hanging out with you all this time? You're looking at Him!" Wouldn't you love to see the expression on Philips face at this point?

If you've seen Jesus, you've seen the God of the universe in human flesh and His purpose was to make God known – to give light to those in darkness – to know the truth and to allow men to be born of God and receive eternal life.

VI. Jesus created and sustains the universe

Colossians 1:16-18

The Son is the image of the invisible God, the firstborn over all creation. For by Him all things were created: things in heaven and on earth, visible and invisible, whether thrones or powers or rulers or authorities; all things have been created by Him and for Him. He is before all things, and in Him all things hold together. And He is the head of the body, the church; He is the beginning and the firstborn from among the dead, so that in everything He might have the supremacy.

In this passage, Paul states that Jesus is the image of the invisible God which we've already discussed. If you've seen Jesus, you've seen God. For by Him, all things were created, things in heaven and on earth. Jesus created things that are visible, and those that are invisible. Invisible things would include gravity, space, atoms, electrons and all spiritual beings. It also claims that in Him, all things hold together. Jesus is the force that holds electrons in their orbit and keeps the world from flying apart. Pretty amazing carpenter wouldn't you agree? Now let's see that the Bible claims that Jesus has authority over the spiritual world and watch the Demon's reaction to Him.

Mark 1:21-28

They went to Capernaum, and when the Sabbath came, Jesus went into the synagogue and began to teach. The people were amazed at his teaching, because he taught them as one who had authority, not as the teachers of the law. Just then a man in their synagogue who was possessed by an evil spirit cried out, "What do you want with us, Jesus of Nazareth? Have you come to destroy us? I know who you are—the Holy One of God!" "Be quiet,"said Jesus sternly. "Come out of Him!"The evil spirit shook the man violently and came out of Him with a shriek.

The people were all so amazed that they asked each other, "What is this? A new teaching—and with authority! He even gives orders to evil spirits and they obey Him."News about Him spread quickly over the whole region of Galilee.

Notice what the evil spirit said? He knew Jesus' name, he knew He had the power to destroy him and called Jesus *"The Holy One of God!"*

Mark 5:1-13

They went across the lake to the region of the Gerasenes. When Jesus got out of the boat, a man with an evil spirit came from the tombs to meet Him. This man lived in the tombs, and no one could bind Him anymore, not even with a chain. For he had often been chained hand and foot, but he tore the chains apart and broke the irons on his feet. No one was strong enough to subdue Him. Night and day among the tombs and in the hills he would cry out and cut Himself with stones.

When he saw Jesus from a distance, he ran and fell on his knees in front of Him. He shouted at the top of his voice, "What do you want with me, Jesus, Son of the Most High God? In God's name don't torture me!" For Jesus had said to Him, "Come out of this man, you evil spirit!"

Then Jesus asked Him, "What is your name?""My name is Legion," he replied, "for we are many." And he begged Jesus again and again not to send them out of the area.

A large herd of pigs was feeding on the nearby hillside. The demons begged Jesus, "Send us among the pigs; allow us to go into them." He gave them permission, and the impure spirits came out and went into the pigs. The herd, about two thousand in number, rushed down the steep bank into the lake and was drowned.

It's interesting to observe in these two occurrences that the spirit is referred to in the plural *"US."* In this second occurrence the demon said his name was Legion. A Roman Legion was comprised of 10 Cohorts, or about 5,000 men. This man was possessed by thousands, possibly 5,000 demons. We can assume there were at least 2,000 since they possessed about 2,000 pigs and apparently drove them immediately insane! This demon, or at least the spokesman for them, begged Jesus not to send them out of the area, again acknowledging Jesus' power and authority to torment or punish them.

In 2 Peter 2:4 it says, *"For if God did not spare angels when they sinned, but sent them to hell, (tartarus) putting them in chains of darkness to be held for judgment."* This word *hell* in this passage is not the final lake of fire (Gahenna) that has been prepared for the devil and his angels, (Matthew 25:41). This is the word *tartarus* which apparently is a temporary prison for demonic beings to be held until the final judgment day. These demons knew Jesus had the power to cast them into this torment before their final and ultimate condemnation in hell.

Hell is not a fun place over which Satan is the master of ceremonies and all the exciting rebellious people go to hang out and party. This lie has been fed to people and they don't take hell as seriously as they should. In these passages we learn that the demonic world is terrified of hell and knows that it is Jesus who has authority to sentence them to an eternity described as burning sulfur, outer darkness where there will be wailing and gnashing of teeth in severe torture.

> *Matthew 8:23-27*
>
> *When He got into the boat, His disciples followed Him. And behold, there arose a great storm on the sea, so that the boat was being covered with the waves; but Jesus Himself was asleep. And they came to Him and woke Him, saying, "Save us, Lord; we are perishing!" He said to them, "Why are you afraid, you men of little faith?" Then He got up and rebuked the winds and the sea, and it became perfectly calm. The men were amazed, and said, "What kind of a man is this, that even the winds and the sea obey Him?"*

Here we have record of Jesus and His disciples being in a boat on the Sea of Galilee. A great storm arose and these seasoned fishermen were afraid and cried out for Jesus to save them! He was amazed at their lack of trust in Him and then He got up and rebuked the storm and immediately it became perfectly calm. They were amazed at His power and authority. Not only do the demons obey but the physical elements also. The reason? The Bible claims that Jesus is the creator and sustainer of the spiritual and physical universe. He speaks; they obey!

VII. Jesus' death can pay for all sin

In this section, we want to explore the story and reason for redemption. Sin is a big deal! It's much bigger than you realize!

> *Romans 3:23 for all have sinned and fall short of the glory of God*

> *Romans 6:23 for the wages of sin is death, but the free gift of God is eternal life in Christ Jesus, our Lord*

These passages reveal the fundamental reason why God became flesh – sin! All have sinned and the penalty for a single sin is capital punishment from the judgment tribunal of heaven. I want you to consider the following reasoning.

How many people have sinned? The Bible says all, including you. What penalty does a single sin have? The penalty is capital punishment – death. One single sin, regardless of how big or small we may *think* it is carries a mandatory minimum sentence of death. Eve only took one bite of fruit, what's the big deal? The big deal is that there is no little sin, because there is no little God to sin against and every sin is against God holiness and His perfect law.

Let's assume that you started knowingly sinning at age ten. You were morally, emotionally, and intellectually capable of sin and knew you were doing it. You might cheat on a test in school or disobey your parents, or fight with a sibling and lie about it. You might covet your friends' bike or hate a bully at school. Do you think it could be reasonable to commit three small sins a day? Sure! If you commit three sins a day over a year, that would be approximately one thousand sins a year. If you did one thousand sins a year for thirty years, that's thirty thousand capital offences on your record.

OK, now you're a felon guilty of thirty thousand capital crimes and every one of them is on video. Let me ask you a question. Think about this. "If you murdered a person, how many people would you have to *not murder* to pay for that one murder? How many little old ladies would you have to help across the street to erase that murder from your record? How much money would you have to give to charity to make that murder OK?" You can't undo it, right? Once you commit a capital crime, you will always be guilty of that crime regardless of how much good you do from that point forward. This is why the Bible says

> **What penalty does a single sin have? The penalty is capital punishment – death. One single sin, regardless of how big or small we may *think* it is carries a mandatory minimum sentence of death.**

that we cannot be saved by good works or *doing a little religion!* Still think you're good enough to go to heaven by your own goodness? You aren't! No one is! One sin, just like one murder, demands capital punishment – death! And we each have thousands!

Now let's examine this dilemma from God's perspective. We know from the Bible that God is love. However, we also know that God is just and will always do the right thing. He will judge the world righteously, truthfully and fairly and will show no favoritism. Let's assume that Hitler was given a trial for his atrocities and found guilty. How would you react if the judge sentenced Him with a fifty dollar fine, released him and said, "Next case please?" You would be outraged, and justifiably so. That judge did a terrible injustice to the dignity of the law. The penalty must match the crime and the penalty for sin is death!

If God is just, fair, and unbiased, can He overlook the thousands of capital crimes on your record without Himself becoming unjust? No! Can God just sweep your crimes under the carpet and pretend to look the other way? No! We are all guilty of sin and God will carry out the penalty for every one of those sins because He's fair and just! "For the wrath of God is being revealed from heaven against all the ungodliness and unrighteousness of men," (Romans 1:18). So how does Jesus' death fit into this picture?

Romans 5:8-10

*But God demonstrates His own love toward us, in that while we were yet sinners, <u>Christ died for us</u>. Much more then, <u>having now been justified by His blood,</u> **we shall be saved from the wrath of God** <u>through Him</u>. For if while we were enemies we were reconciled to God through the death of His Son, much more, having been reconciled, we shall be saved by His life.*

God is love, but He's also righteous so the crime of sin and its' penalty cannot be ignored. So, here's what God did. He demonstrated His love for us and sent His own Son in the likeness of sinful man to pay the full penalty for the sin of the world by executing Him to fulfill the law's requirement of capital punishment. He laid upon Jesus the sin of the world and made Him guilty even though He had committed no sin. In that act of dying on our behalf, He offers us free, but conditional, terms of pardon which we'll explore later.

When we accept those terms of pardon, we have been *justified* which is a court term of acquittal. It's actually more than an acquittal. A court in Vancouver, British Columbia did the unthinkable in pronouncing a sentence that had never before been done in a Canadian court. It declared a man *"pardoned and deemed innocent."* Governors have pardoned criminals before but they were never pronounced innocent in the process.

> **If these claims are not true, then there is no way you can remain neutral about this man. You are forced to reject Him as history's greatest hoax and liar, or admit that He is who He claims to be – King of Kings and Lord of Lords!**

This word *justified* means exactly that. It's much more than just being declared *not guilty* or given a stay of execution. When you accept Gods offer He declares you *pardoned and deemed innocent.* A good way to remember *justified* is " *just-as-if-I'd"* never sinned in the first place, therefore I'm innocent and not subject to the penalty of the crime because I am now innocent as though it never happened. When that transaction occurs, the text says, "We shall be saved from the wrath of God." But you must accept the terms of this pardon and understand that you are never good enough to deserve it. But there are terms!

I saw a great commercial on TV years ago that illustrates this idea perfectly. The camera zooms into a prison cell where a death-row criminal is nervously pacing back and forth wringing his hands in agonizing anticipation. The clock ticks one second at a time – tick, tick, tick as the sweat runs from his brow. He's moments away from being executed. Meanwhile at the end of the hall the guards are preparing the electric chair for his eminent execution. They tighten the wires, adjust the straps. Then you hear steps echoing though the hollow hallway and the guard opens the creaking cell door. You look into the eyes of the terrified criminal assuming

> God is love, but He's also righteous so the crime of sin and its' penalty cannot be ignored.

it's his time to die and the guard says, "You're free to go." "Free to go," questions the astounded man? "Yes," declares the guard, "Somebody took your place." At that the camera zooms to the electric chair and Jesus' body sits there motionless.

The cross is God carrying out fully His justice for the sin of the entire world. He couldn't and didn't sweep sin under the carpet. He carried out the full weight of His wrath. You either hang on the cross or go to hell to pay for your own sin or somebody else had to take your place. *"It was God's good pleasure to crush Him and lay upon Him the iniquity of us all!"*(Isaiah 53:5-6). And in His wisdom He devised a plan by which He could be just and the justifier of the one who accepts His terms of pardon in Christ. When our sin is removed and we are declared *justified* we are reconciled, and made friends again with God. We were His enemies because of sin and by the death of Christ and our acceptance of His gracious offer, the crimes that separated us have been removed and we are once again made friends – reconciled!

   1 Timothy 2:5-6

For there is one God, and one mediator also between God and men, the man Christ Jesus, who gave Himself as a ransom for all

A mediator is one who brokers a deal between two opposing or estranged parties. This verse tells us that there is only one mediator between God and men and that's the man Jesus who is God in the flesh. He gave Himself as a ransom or payment for all. Now if God accepts only one mediator, what does that says about other men or religions? Are Buddha, Mohammed, Mary, the Pope, the saints, Joseph Smith or even the apostles themselves acceptable mediators? NO! There's only one mediator between God and man – Jesus. That is what these following verses mean. This might offend you, but it's what Jesus claims! Being spiritual or religious won't cut it.

John 14:6

I am the way and the truth and the life. <u>No one comes to the Father except by me.</u>

Acts 4:12

And there is salvation in no one else; <u>for there is no other name under heaven that has been given among men by which we must be saved.</u>"

We're examining what the Bible claims about Jesus. These claims are either true or false. If these claims are not true, then there is no way you can remain neutral about this man. You are forced to reject Him as history's greatest hoax and liar, or admit that He is who He claims to be – King of Kings and Lord of Lords! We'll see if there's enough evidence to believe His claims in our next chapter. His claims are validated by His resurrection from the dead. True or false?

VIII. Jesus rose from the dead and is alive today

Matthew 28:1-10

Now after the Sabbath, as it began to dawn toward the first day of the week, Mary Magdalene and the other Mary came to look at the grave. And behold, a severe earthquake had occurred, for an angel of the Lord descended from heaven and came and rolled away the stone and sat upon it. And his appearance was like lightning and his clothing as white as snow. The guards shook for fear of Him and became like dead men. The angel said to the women, "Do not be afraid; for I know that you are looking for Jesus who has been crucified. He is not here, for He has risen, just as He said. Come; see the place where He was lying. Go quickly and tell His disciples that He has risen from the dead; and behold, He is going ahead of you into Galilee, there you will see Him; behold, I have told you."

And they left the tomb quickly with fear and great joy and ran to report it to His disciples and behold, Jesus met them and greeted them. And they came up and took hold of His feet and worshiped Him. Then Jesus said to them, "Do not be afraid; go and take word to my brethren to leave for Galilee, and there they will see Me."

1 Corinthians 15:3-8

For I delivered to you as of first importance what I also received, that Christ died for our sins according to the Scriptures, and that He was buried, and that He was raised on the

If Jesus didn't actually rise from the dead, the entire Christian faith is a hoax and those who believe this fairy-tale are fools!

third day according to the Scriptures, and that He appeared to Cephas, then to the twelve. After that He appeared to more than five hundred brethren at one time, most of whom remain until now, but some have fallen asleep; then He appeared to James, then to all the apostles; and last of all, He appeared to me also as to one untimely born

These passages claim that Jesus rose from the dead after having been dead for three days. He was apparently seen by many people on several occasions over a forty day period of time. Now this event is really the crux of the matter. It's the proof for the claims made about Him as you will see from this following verse.

1 Corinthians 15:17-19

If Christ has not been raised, your faith is worthless; you are still in your sins. Then those also who have fallen asleep in Christ have perished. If we have hoped in Christ in this life only, we are of all men most to be pitied.

If Jesus really didn't rise from the dead, Christianity collapses in on itself as a pathetic fairy tale promoted by con-men and believed by gullible, superstitious people. We will examine the evidence for the resurrection in our next chapter and see if it is sufficient to intelligently believe.

IX. Jesus will be the judge of the entire world

John 12:48

"He who rejects me and does not receive my sayings, has one who judges Him; the word I spoke is what will condemn Him at the last day."

Here we have a very clear claim by Jesus that those who do not receive Him and His teachings would be condemned on the judgment day.

2 Corinthians 5:10-11

For we must all appear before the judgment seat of Christ, so that each one may be recompensed for his deeds in the body, according to what he has done, whether good or bad. Therefore, knowing the fear of the Lord, we persuade men.

Every person who has lived will be at the judgment seat and Christ will be on the bench. The payment for sin will be extracted and payment required. We will either pay the penalty for our own sin, or we will have accepted the payment of Christ and be declared pardoned and deemed innocent. The following passage shows us what the judgment will look like at the end of the world.

Revelation 20:11-15

Then I saw a great white throne and Him who sat upon it, from whose presence earth and heaven fled away, and no place was found for them. And I saw the dead, the great and the small, standing before the throne, and books were opened; and another book was opened, which is the book of life; and the dead were judged from the things which were written in the books, according to their deeds. And the sea gave up the dead, who were in it, and death and Hades gave up the dead which were in them; and they were judged, every one of them according to their deeds. Then death and Hades were thrown into the lake of fire. This is the second death, the lake of fire. And if anyone's name was not found written in the book of life, he was thrown into the lake of fire.

We see here what is sure to be a terrifying appointment that none of us will miss. Each of us will be there along with the billions of inhabitants of the earth from Adam forward. There are two separate documents that will be opened. The *books,* which are the records of the thoughts and actions of each of us, and *The book of life,* which is the court document listing those whose sins have been paid in full and forgiven. If anyone's name is not found in the book of life, he will receive the just sentence for his own capital crimes and thrown into the lake of fire along with Satan and his angels for whom hell was created. Men made in the image of God were never intended for that horrible destination, but because we sinned and refused to accept God's offer of salvation, that will be the result because the wrath of God is just, fair, and unbiased. We will show in a later chapter how to be in the book of life!

X. Conclusion

As you can see, the Bible makes some incredible claims about Jesus. It claims that He is eternal (from before the beginning of time), that He is God in the flesh, that He created and holds the universe together, and that His death is able to pay for the sins of all men for all time. The Bible also claims that He will be the judge of the world and that every human being will stand before Him and give account of their lives and the sins for which they are guilty.

There are "terms of pardon" or certain conditions that must be met in order to receive the forgiveness of sins and the free gift of God. Just because it's free, doesn't mean it's without conditions. It is God's loving desire and should be ours to be listed in the Book of Life. *"The Lord is* *not slow in keeping his promise, as some understand slowness. Instead he is patient with you, <u>not wanting anyone to perish</u>, but everyone to come to repentance. But the day of the Lord will come like a thief, and then the heavens will pass away with a roar, and the earth and its works will be burned up. Since all these things are to be destroyed in this way, what sort of people ought you to be... Therefore beloved, since you look for these things, be diligent to be found in Him in peace, spotless and blameless," (2 Peter 3:9-14).* We will examine those terms of pardon in a later chapter. Be certain that you meet His terms of pardon in Christ!

The Bible claims that Jesus rose from the dead after having been dead for three days. This event, as you will see, is the crux of the matter. Did He really rise again, or is He like other religious leaders of the past - still dead in the grave? If He is still in the grave, then all of His claims and the entire Bible are false. If, however, there is sufficient evidence to show that He is alive and did rise from the dead, then His claims are true.

Chapter 3 - Evidence for Christ's Resurrection

 All the claims that the Bible make about Jesus are either true or false. The credibility of the Christian faith depends upon whether or not Jesus actually came out of the grave as He claimed He would. If Christ did not rise from the dead, the entire Christian faith is discredited, the Bible is false, and those who follow Jesus as a religious leader are fools (1 Corinthians 15:17-19). However, if the resurrection is true, then Jesus is Lord and all of the claims about Him in the Bible are absolutely true.

In this chapter, we will examine four witnesses for cross examination. It is your task to be a jury member and listen to the testimony presented. This type of deliberation based upon testimony is what our court system is built upon. No jury member ever witnesses the crime committed. They made their decision upon testimony given.

A jury member listens to evidence and testimony presented and must answer the question of legitimacy of the testimony in his own mind. Is the witness credible? Does he have a motive for lying? What impact does his testimony have on his own life if he is telling the truth? Does telling the truth benefit or harm the witness's reputation, his career, or his safety and well-being? You've heard of people afraid to tell the truth at the trial of a mob boss for fear of their own life. Sometimes telling the truth is disadvantageous for the witness. These are the type of questions with which jurors struggle when listening to testimony.

> You are in the jury box and you MUST make a decision... True or False? Dead or Alive? You decide based on the evidence you hear.

Ultimately, you must decide for yourself if there is sufficient reason to believe the resurrection claim based upon the evidence in existence and the testimony presented. You must weigh the evidence and testimony against credibility and motive. Let's call the first witness to the stand!

I. Witness #1: The remarkable change in the life of Christ's disciples

The week of Jesus' trial and execution was one of the most turbulent times in history. He had become well-known throughout all of Israel as a great teacher. He had performed countless miracles and masses followed Him to the point of going days without food just to hear Him teach. The Jewish leaders had been trying to kill Him for over a year, but fear of an upheaval from His followers made them hesitate lest they incite a national riot.

The Romans had enough of this Jewish foolishness! From Caesar all the way down the chain of command to the local governor Pontius Pilate, there was a growing hatred for these obnoxious and irritating Jews. Now Pilate was forced by political pressure to kill Christ in a lame attempt to appease these complaining Jewish leaders. He thought this might satisfy them for a period of time so he could be through with them. But the pressure was just about to rupture more than he could have imagined!

Jesus' followers scattered like rats on a sinking ship the day of His unlawful arrest and mock trials. All, except His mom, a few other women and His best friend and first cousin John remained during the entirety of the ordeal. Their hopes of overthrowing Rome and restoring the nation of Israel to her glory days had been shattered with the murder of their leader. The shock and disillusion of His once-hopeful followers would have been as traumatic an event as the assassination of John Kennedy or Martin Luther King. Their leader brutally slain and all their hopes buried in a grave. But that Sunday morning things began to change drastically. Some women who were His closest followers experience something unbelievable- an empty tomb!

Luke 24:10-12

"It was Mary Magdalene, Joanna, Mary the mother of James, and the others with them who told this to the apostles. But they did not believe the women, because their words seemed to them like nonsense. Peter, however, got up and ran to the tomb. Bending over, he saw the strips of linen, lying by themselves, and he went away wondering to Himself what had happened."

I want you to put yourselves in the story. As a child, I still remember vividly the day Kennedy was buried in Arlington Cemetery. The entire nation and most of the world was in a state of deep mourning just like Jesus' followers would have been. Now, can you imagine the reaction if three days later someone came running to your house and told you they had just seen John Kennedy and talked with Him and he wanted to meet with you? You saw him buried! And now some hysterical women are telling you that they had just seen him alive? That's what is happening in this story. Would you listen to hysterical women if you'd seen him buried with your own eyes?

The women's' words seem like nonsense – and rightfully so. They saw their leader brutally murdered and buried and two Roman guards placed by the tomb. Dead men don't just come back to life and crawl out of their own tomb, especially those who had been brutally tortured and their bodies mutilated beyond recognition. The apostles' first reaction was unbelief. The story was absurd! Insulting! But Peter remembered some amazing things Jesus had done and upon hearing this story jumps up and runs frantically to the tomb, looks inside and sees the burial clothes lying uninhabited as his jaw drops and his heart pounds! He doesn't believe what he just heard, and can't believe what he now sees. Things are about to change!

> The women's' words seem like nonsense – and rightfully so. They saw their leader brutally murdered and buried and two Roman guards placed by the tomb. Dead men don't just come back to life and crawl out of their own tomb, especially those who had been brutally tortured and their bodies mutilated beyond recognition.

Jesus appeared to His disciples later that evening, but Thomas, one of the twelve, was not with them. He wouldn't see Jesus until eight days later. Now remember that you're a jury member as you consider all of the things you are hearing. Ten of the disciples claim they saw Jesus alive that Sunday evening after first hearing the report from the women earlier that morning. The Jewish leaders were still in a heated fury after killing Jesus – the ring leader of this Messiah Movement. They supposed they had squelched the movement by His crucifixion, but His disciples were still afraid for their own lives, so they lay low. After their initial unbelief of this resurrection story, they claim they met with Jesus alive for the first time that very evening. Here's their testimony.

John 20:24-29

But Thomas, one of the twelve, called Didymus, was not with them when Jesus came. So the other disciples were saying to Him, "We have seen the Lord!" But he said to them, "Unless I see in His hands the imprint of the nails, and put my finger into the place of the nails, and put my hand into His side, I will not believe."

After eight days His disciples were again inside and Thomas with them. Jesus came, the doors having been shut, and stood in their midst and said, "Peace be with you." Then He said to Thomas, "Reach here with your finger, and see My hands; and reach here your hand and put it into My side; and do not be unbelieving, but believing." Thomas answered and said to Him, "My Lord and my God!" Jesus said to Him, "Because you have seen Me, have you believed? Blessed are they who did not see, and yet believed."

Jesus' closest friends are now changing their story, and fairly quickly. Ten of them changed from thinking the resurrection story was nonsense, to claiming that they met with Jesus the evening of that Sunday when he came back to life. A week later, Thomas, another of the original twelve, changed his mind and accepted that Jesus was alive. Of course, Judas was no longer part of the group.

Not only did his closest followers change their attitude shortly, but this resurrection message became the driving force behind this mission that now consumed their lives. Look at the content of their public messages. The first public proclamation was on the Jewish festival of Pentecost in Jerusalem where tens of thousands of Jewish pilgrims had gathered for the annual celebration of Passover and Pentecost – a fifty day long yearly convention of sorts. Peters' sermon is here recorded.

> *Acts 2:22-24*
>
> *'This man was handed over to you by God's deliberate plan and foreknowledge; and you, with the help of wicked men, put Him to death by nailing Him to the cross. "Fellow Israelites, listen to this: Jesus of Nazareth was a man accredited by God to you by miracles, wonders and signs, which God did among you through Him, as you yourselves know. <u>But God raised Him from the dead, freeing Him from the agony of death, because it was impossible for death to keep its hold on Him.</u> '*
>
> *Acts 2:32*
>
> *This Jesus God raised up again, to which we are all witnesses.*

At this gathering, approximately three thousand people believed the testimony about the resurrection of Jesus and were baptized. This was the beginning of a fast-growing movement and it is Jesus' closest friends who are proclaiming publicly that Jesus had been raised from the dead and they actually ate and drank with Him after He came back to life.

> *Acts 4:33*
>
> *And with great power the apostles were giving testimony to the resurrection of the Lord Jesus*

The message of Jesus' resurrection continues to be the theme of their message, even ten years later when we review the record of Peter's message to the first non-Jewish audience.

> *Acts 10:39-43*
>
> *We are witnesses of all the things He did both in the land of the Jews and in Jerusalem. They also put Him to death by hanging*

Him on a cross. God raised Him up on the third day and granted that He become visible, not to all the people, but to witnesses who were chosen beforehand by God, that is, to us who ate and drank with Him after He arose from the dead. And He ordered us to preach to the people, and solemnly to testify that this is the One who has been appointed by God as Judge of the living and the dead. Of Him all the prophets bear witness that through His name everyone who believes in Him receives forgiveness of sins."

As a jury member I want you to consider a few important facts here. First, his closest friends saw Jesus brutally tortured, murdered and buried. The first report from some women that He was alive seemed to them absurd. They claim, however that they met with Him alive that Sunday evening. They shared this meeting with Thomas, who was not with them, but he disbelieved their story until, according to his testimony, he saw Jesus alive eight days later. This resurrection story now becomes the theme of their preaching and they are claiming that Jesus was raised from the dead and they had eaten with Him.

> **People lie for all kinds of reasons; to save their reputation or their life. Some lie for money, fame or pleasure. Are these guys lying? What would their motive be? You're the jury member.. think about it.**

But people lie, don't they? Why would they fabricate a story such as this and why so quickly? They transition from being frightened skeptics to believers in a few hours, then publicly proclaiming this story a little over a month later. Perhaps they are motivated by money, fame or even embarrassment – not wanting to look like fools for following a leader who couldn't produce what He'd claimed. As you deliberate, take these things into consideration, and let's examine those motives as we continue to uncover the story.

This story about the resurrection of Jesus and the claim that He is the Son of God starts to spread rapidly throughout the region. Now let's see how far his friends are willing to take this story. Let's test their motives against verbal opposition, physical torture, and imprisonment and see if their story remains intact.

Acts 4:15-21

*But when they had ordered them to leave the Council,
they began to confer with one another, saying, "What shall we
do with these men? For the fact that a noteworthy miracle has
taken place through them is apparent to all who live in
Jerusalem, and we cannot deny it. But so that it will not spread
any further among the people, let us warn them to speak no
longer to any man in this name." And when they had summoned
them, they commanded them not to speak or teach at all in the
name of Jesus. But Peter and John answered and said to them,
"Whether it is right in the sight of God to give heed to you rather
than to God, you be the judge; for we cannot stop speaking
about what we have seen and heard." When they had
threatened them further, they let them go (finding no basis on
which to punish them)*

The heat of opposition is beginning. The Jewish Council doesn't want
this Jesus movement to continue, so they drag the opinion leaders,
Peter and John, into a meeting and warn them to stop spreading this
message. Their reply, "We cannot (and will not) stop speaking about
what we have seen and heard." They claim they saw Jesus alive, and ate
with Him. But the Jewish leaders will not tolerate this foolishness, and
have these trouble-makers thrown in prison.

Acts 5:28-33; 40-42

*But someone came and reported to them, "The men whom you
put in prison are standing in the temple and teaching the
people!"Then the captain went along with the officers
and proceeded to bring them back without violence (for they
were afraid of the people, that they might be stoned). When they
had brought them, they stood them before the Council. The high
priest questioned them, saying, "We gave you strict orders not to
continue teaching in this name, and yet, you have filled
Jerusalem with your teaching and intend to bring this man's
blood upon us." But Peter and the apostles answered, "We must
obey God rather than men. The God of our fathers raised up
Jesus, whom you had put to death by hanging Him on a cross. He*

is the one whom God exalted to His right hand as a Prince and a Savior, to grant repentance to Israel, and forgiveness of sins. And we are witnesses of these things; and so is the Holy Spirit, whom God has given to those who obey Him." But when they heard this, they were cut to the quick and intended to kill them...after calling the apostles in, they flogged them and ordered them not to speak in the name of Jesus, and then released them. So they went on their way from the presence of the Council, rejoicing that they had been considered worthy to suffer shame for His name. And every day, in the temple and from house to house, they kept right on teaching and preaching Jesus as the Christ.

The Jewish leaders now imprison the apostles for filling Jerusalem with this story. But after being released from prison, what do the apostles do? They go out into the streets and continue preaching that Jesus rose from the dead and is the Messiah. The Council drags them in again and wants to kill them, but they are advised against that by a more sensible member named Gamaliel. Instead, they torture them by beating their naked backs.

Flogging was horribly cruel and painful. However even after experiencing that intensity of torture, the apostles' claims about the resurrection of Jesus do not change. They continue every day publicly and from house to house preaching that Jesus is the Messiah and was raised from the dead.

Remember, as a jury member, you're looking at not only the message, but the motive. Why are they continuing to tell this story when the opposition and personal cost is that extensive? You have to ask yourself if they would continue against this type of opposition if they knew they were telling a lie. I can't imagine it myself. Someone said that there is no honor among thieves. When someone's freedom or personal well-being is being threatened, someone is going to "spill the beans" and tell what's really happening. If you watched your friend's back being beaten and knew this was all a big lie, don't you think someone would come forward to stop this insanity? When it's your turn to be beaten, if you know it's a lie, you're going to tell!

 I think you'd have to logically conclude that these men were preaching this message about Jesus being raised because they actually believed it happened, and there was no ulterior motive behind their teaching. In spite of the opposition, imprisonment and torture, their story never once deviated.

Now we are going to see that these men and other followers of Christ are dying for their testimony about Jesus' resurrection.

> *Acts 12:1-2*
>
> *"Now about that time Herod the king stretched forth his hands to persecute certain of the church. And he killed James the brother of John with the sword"*
>
> *Acts 8:1-4*
>
> *"And they stoned Stephen, calling upon God, and saying, Lord Jesus, receive my spirit.*
>
> *And he kneeled down, and cried with a loud voice, Lord; lay not this sin to their charge. And when he had said this, he fell asleep.*
>
> *And Saul was consenting unto his death. And at that time there was a great persecution against the church which was at Jerusalem; and they were all scattered abroad throughout the regions of Judaea and Samaria, except the apostles.*
>
> *And devout men carried Stephen to his burial, and made great lamentation over Him.*
>
> *As for Saul, he made havoc of the church, entering into every house, and haling men and women committed them to prison. Therefore they that were scattered abroad went everywhere preaching the word"*

As we've already mentioned, people will die for something they believe is true. But I think you'd agree that no one in his right mind would die for something he knew was a lie. The only reason Stephen and James and many others were persecuted, imprisoned and killed is that they said Jesus had been raised from the dead. They would have known if that was or was not a lie.

The followers and personal friends of Jesus lost their businesses, their reputations, some lost their families, their credibility, their personal well-being, and even their lives for their testimony that they ate and drank with Jesus after he rose from the dead. Other than the resurrection itself, can you think of another *reasonable* explanation for why they would make this claim? I've never heard of one!

> *Would you die for something that you KNEW was a lie? Think about it. You're on the jury!*

II. Witness #2: The changed life of Saul of Tarsus

We've been introduced to this man Saul of Tarsus, who was a prominent Jewish leader, a member of the prestigious Pharisees – a highly orthodox sect of the Jews. He was well connected religiously and politically and acquired letters authorizing him to lead a group of loyalists to destroy this so-called Christian cult. They murdered Stephen and began arresting both men and women and throwing them into prison. The opposition to the Christian church and its heretical teaching about Jesus' resurrection was more than they could tolerate! It had to be destroyed!

While on a search and destroy mission en route to Damascus, something altered the course of Saul's entire life. Watch what happened.

> *Acts 7:54 - 8:3*
>
> *Meanwhile, Saul was still breathing out murderous threats against the Lord's disciples. He went to the high priest and asked Him for letters to the synagogues in Damascus, so that if he found any there who belonged to the Way, whether men or women, he might take them as prisoners to Jerusalem. As he neared Damascus on his journey, suddenly a light from heaven*

flashed around Him. He fell to the ground and heard a voice say to Him, "Saul, Saul, why do you persecute me?"

"Who are you, Lord?" Saul asked. "I am Jesus, whom you are persecuting," he replied. "Now get up and go into the city, and you will be told what you must do."

The men traveling with Saul stood there speechless; they heard the sound but did not see anyone. Saul got up from the ground, but when he opened his eyes he could see nothing. So they led Him by the hand into Damascus. For three days he was blind, and did not eat or drink anything" (Acts 9:1-9).

Saul will later tell in his own words this event. Max Lucado says of this encounter that, "God placed scales so thick on Saul's eyes that the only place he could look was inside Himself." He prays! He doesn't eat or drink for three whole days. His life and beliefs have been shaken to the core of his being. Totally confused and disoriented, Saul must have been crying for understanding about what just happened to him and pleading for forgiveness from the God of his fathers. Then a Jewish man comes reluctantly to Saul with a message from heaven.

Acts 9:17-29

Then Ananias went to the house and entered it. Placing his hands on Saul, he said, "Brother Saul, the Lord—Jesus, who appeared to you on the road as you were coming here—has sent me so that you may see again and be filled with the Holy Spirit." Immediately, something like scales fell from Saul's eyes, and he could see again. He got up and was baptized, and after taking some food, he regained his strength.

Saul spent several days with the disciples in Damascus. At once he began to preach in the synagogues that Jesus is the Son of God. All those who heard Him were astonished and asked, "Isn't he the man who raised havoc in Jerusalem among those who call on this name? And hasn't he come here to take them as prisoners to the chief priests?" Yet Saul grew more and more powerful and baffled the Jews living in Damascus by proving that Jesus is the Messiah.

After many days had gone by, there was a conspiracy among the Jews to kill Him, but Saul learned of their plan. Day and night they kept close watch on the city gates in order to kill Him. But his followers took Him by night and lowered Him in a basket through an opening in the wall.

When he came to Jerusalem, he tried to join the disciples, but they were all afraid of Him, not believing that he really was a disciple. But Barnabas took Him and brought Him to the apostles. He told them how Saul on his journey had seen the Lord and that the Lord had spoken to Him, and how in Damascus he had preached fearlessly in the name of Jesus. So Saul stayed with them and moved about freely in Jerusalem, speaking boldly in the name of the Lord. He talked and debated with the Hellenistic Jews, but they tried to kill Him" .

This was a moment in time that forever changed Saul. After a brief recovery and being baptized he immediately begins preaching in the Jewish Synagogue in Damascus proclaiming that Jesus really was the Christ. Can you imagine what his first sermon must have been like? He baffled the Jews and proved that Jesus really was the Christ and had been raised from the dead. And instead of cheering Him on and listening, they try to kill Him. The conversion of Saul would be parallel to Ben Laden becoming an American Patriot. That's how significant this man's encounter with Jesus was and it changed the history of the world as you will soon discover.

Years after his conversion, Saul, who became the Apostle Paul (Saul is his Hebrew name, Paul his Greek name) requested to speak to a group of Hebrews in Jerusalem. Here now is the story in Saul's own words:

Acts 22:1-22

"Brothers and fathers, listen now to my defense." When they heard Him speak to them in Aramaic, they became very quiet.

Then Paul said: "I am a Jew, born in Tarsus of Cilicia, but brought up in this city. I studied under Gamaliel and was thoroughly trained in the law of our ancestors. I was just as zealous for God as any of you are today. I persecuted the followers of this Way to their death, arresting both men and women and throwing them into prison, as the high priest and all the Council can themselves testify. I even obtained letters from them to their associates in Damascus, and went there to bring these people as prisoners to Jerusalem to be punished.

"About noon as I came near Damascus, suddenly a bright light from heaven flashed around me. I fell to the ground and heard a voice say to me, 'Saul! Saul! Why do you persecute me?' 8"'Who are you, Lord?' I asked.

"'I am Jesus of Nazareth, whom you are persecuting, 'he replied. My companions saw the light, but they did not understand the voice of Him who was speaking to me.

"'What shall I do, Lord?' I asked. "'Get up, 'the Lord said, 'and go into Damascus. There you will be told all that you have been assigned to do.' My companions led me by the hand into Damascus, because the brilliance of the light had blinded me.

"A man named Ananias came to see me. He was a devout observer of the law and highly respected by all the Jews living there. He stood beside me and said, 'Brother Saul, receive your sight!' And at that very moment I was able to see Him.

"Then he said: 'The God of our ancestors has chosen you to know his will and to see the Righteous One and to hear words from his mouth. You will be his witness to all people of what you have seen and heard. And now what are you waiting for? Get up, be baptized and wash your sins away, calling on his name.'

"When I returned to Jerusalem and was praying at the temple, I fell into a trance and saw the Lord speaking to me. 'Quick! 'He said, 'Leave Jerusalem immediately, because the people here will not accept your testimony about me.'" 'Lord,' I replied, 'these people know that I went from one synagogue to another to imprison and beat those who believe in you. And when the blood of your martyr Stephen was shed, I stood there giving my *approval and guarding the clothes of those who were killing Him.'*

"Then the Lord said to me, 'Go; I will send you far away to the Gentiles.' " The crowd listened to Paul until he said this. Then they raised their voices and shouted, "Rid the earth of Him! He's not fit to live!".

Saul became the apostle Paul (Acts 13:9) and eventually wrote 13 of the New Testament books. He became history's most powerful advocate for Christianity and based his mission on the resurrection of Christ. This is his message to the churches in the region of Galatia written about 50 AD.

Galatians 1:11-24

I want you to know, brothers and sisters that the gospel I preached is not of human origin. I did not receive it from any man, nor was I taught it; rather, I received it by revelation from Jesus Christ.

For you have heard of my previous way of life in Judaism, how intensely I persecuted the church of God and tried to destroy it. I was advancing in Judaism beyond many of my own age among my people and was extremely zealous for the traditions of my fathers. But when God, who set me apart from my mothers' womb and called me by his grace, was pleased to reveal his Son in me so that I might preach Him among the Gentiles, my immediate response was not to consult any human being. I did not go up to Jerusalem to see those who were apostles before I was, but I went into Arabia. Later I returned to Damascus.

Then after three years, I went up to Jerusalem to get acquainted with Cephas and stayed with Him fifteen days. I saw none of the other apostles—only James, the Lords' brother. I assure you before God that what I am writing you is no lie.

Then I went to Syria and Cilicia. I was personally unknown to the churches of Judea that are in Christ. They only heard the report:

"The man who formerly persecuted us is now preaching the faith he once tried to destroy." And they praised God because of me.

On Paul's second missionary journey, he visited Athens Greece and spoke on the Areopagus, a gathering place on Mars Hill where citizens met to discuss the latest ideas and philosophies. He noticed the statues to all the Greek idols and in this speech he anchors his reasoning in the resurrection of Jesus.

Acts 17:23-34

For as I walked around and looked carefully at your objects of worship, I even found an altar with this inscription: to an unknown god. So you are ignorant of the very thing you worship—and this is what I am going to proclaim to you.

"The God who made the world and everything in it is the Lord of heaven and earth and does not live in temples built by human hands. And he is not served by human hands, as if he needed anything. Rather, He Himself gives everyone life and breath and everything else. From one man he made all the nations, that they should inhabit the whole earth; and he marked out their appointed times in history and the boundaries of their lands. God did this so that they would seek Him and perhaps reach out for Him and find Him, though he is not far from any one of us. 'For in Him we live and move and have our being.' As some of your own poets have said, 'We are his offspring.'

> **Paul in this speech anchors his reasoning in the resurrection of Jesus.**

"Therefore since we are Gods' offspring, we should not think that the divine being is like gold or silver or stone—an image made by human design and skill. In the past God overlooked such ignorance, but now he commands all people everywhere to repent. For he has set a day when he will judge the world with justice by the man he has appointed. He has given proof of this to everyone by raising Him from the dead."

When they heard about the resurrection of the dead, some of them sneered, but others said, "We want to hear you again on this subject." At that, Paul left the Council. Some of the people became followers of Paul and believed. Among them was Dionysius, a member of the Areopagus, also a woman named Damaris, and a number of others.

Please note how Paul argues that we are created in the image of God and not in the image of statues or things made from humans. God has set a judgment day and has given proof of this by raising Jesus from the dead. But who changed Paul's (Saul's) mind? Who or what changed him from being a self righteous terrorist focused on eliminating Christianity to now being the most forceful spokesman for the resurrection of Jesus as the only hope for the salvation of the human race? Obviously, Christians didn't change his mind – he was persecuting them. It's not logical to assume that the Jews somehow convinced him. Paul himself claims that he saw Jesus alive on the road to Damascus and that He was in fact the Messiah, and the Son of God.

Other than the resurrection itself; what reasonable explanation can you think of that would cause an important, influential, intelligent man like Saul of Tarsus to change his beliefs and jeopardize his life and his freedom?

His conversion did not come without great cost to Him, financially, socially, religiously and as it related to his own safety. He wrote to the church in the city of Philippi, the first Christian church on the European continent, that knowing Christ and the power of his resurrection was far more valuable than anything this life could possibly offer.

Philippians 3:4-11

If someone else thinks they have reasons to put confidence in the flesh, I have more: circumcised on the eighth day, of the people of Israel, of the tribe of Benjamin, a Hebrew of Hebrews; in regard to the law, a Pharisee; as for zeal, persecuting the church; as for righteousness based on the law, faultless.

But whatever were gains to me I now consider loss for the sake of Christ. What is more, I consider everything a loss because of the surpassing worth of knowing Christ Jesus my Lord, for whose sake I have lost all things. I consider them garbage, that I may *gain Christ and be found in Him, not having a righteousness of my own that comes from the law, but that which is through faith in Christ—the righteousness that comes from God on the basis of faith. <u>I want to know Christ—yes, to know the power of his resurrection and participation in his sufferings, becoming like Him in his death, and so, somehow, attaining to the resurrection from the dead.</u>*

Other than the resurrection itself, what reasonable explanation can you think of that would cause an important, influential, intelligent man like Saul of Tarsus to change his beliefs and jeopardize his life and his freedom? I have yet to hear a plausible explanation other than he must have seen Jesus alive as he claims.

III. Witness #3: The Jews could not produce a dead body

Jesus was killed on the Passover in the Jewish calendar. This was a day set aside by Moses to remember Israel's deliverance from Egypt and God sparing those who had the blood of the Passover lamb over their doors. Jesus was to be the Passover lamb that spares those who are covered in his blood and protected from the judgment to come.

Pentecost (meaning "fifty") was a holiday known as the Festival of Weeks, or, more simply, Weeks (*Shavuot* in Hebrew). This name comes from an expression in Leviticus 23:16 which instruct people to count seven weeks or "fifty days" from the end of Passover to the beginning of the next holiday (*pentekonta hemeras* in the ancient Greek translation of the Hebrew Scripture).

Pentecost (*havuot*) was the second great feast in Israel's yearly cycle of holy days. It was originally a harvest festival (Exodus 23:16). Over time it became a day to commemorate the giving of the law on Mt. Sinai. Jewish pilgrims would travel to Jerusalem to celebrate the Passover and stay for Pentecost with friends or relatives. It was a time of celebration to remember that God delivered His people and gave them Torah. This year, Pentecost would mark the beginning of something totally new – including a new Covenant and the end of the old.

The political and religious climate was more than tense this year. Jewish tensions were intense and the Romans tolerance for this annoying group of people was nearing an end and would ultimately climax with the total destruction of Jerusalem in 40 years. This Jesus movement was still the talk of the town and it was about to get a whole lot bigger this Pentecost! And there was nothing the Jews could do to stop it. If only they could produce a corpse of this man Jesus, they could put an end to this movement.

Jesus told his followers and in particular His apostles to wait in Jerusalem for what was about to happen. We'll look at more of the details in just a bit, but I want to focus on the witness at hand. We're looking at the fact that the Jews could not produce a dead corpse to disprove the resurrection claim. And look what Peter's message is to this multitude of Jews on that day.

> *Acts 2:31-41*
>
> *Seeing what was to come, he (David) spoke of the resurrection of the Messiah, that he was not abandoned to the realm of the dead, nor did his body see decay. God has raised this Jesus to life, and we are all witnesses of it. "Therefore let all Israel be assured of this: God has made this Jesus, whom you crucified, both Lord and Messiah."*
>
> *When the people heard this, they were cut to the heart and said to Peter and the other apostles, "Brothers, what shall we do?"*
>
> *Peter replied, "Repent and be baptized, every one of you, in the name of Jesus Christ for the forgiveness of your sins. And you will receive the gift of the Holy Spirit. The promise is for you and your children and for all who are far off—for all whom the Lord our God will call."*
>
> *With many other words he warned them; and he pleaded with them, "Save yourselves from this corrupt generation." Those who accepted his message were baptized, and about three thousand were added to their number that day.*

The resurrection of Jesus is the central theme of the Christian message from here on and the Jewish leaders don't like it one bit!

Acts 4:1-2

The priests and the captain of the temple guard and the Sadducees came up to Peter and John while they were speaking to the people. They were greatly disturbed because the apostles were teaching the people, proclaiming in Jesus the resurrection of the dead.

Ten years after Pentecost, Peter was invited to house of an Italian Military officer's house to tell the message of Christ.

Acts 10:39-43

We are witnesses of everything he did in the country of the Jews and in Jerusalem. They killed Him by hanging Him on a cross, but God raised Him from the dead on the third day and caused Him to be seen. He was not seen by all the people, but by witnesses whom God had already chosen—by us who ate and drank with Him after he rose from the dead. He commanded us to preach to the people and to testify that he is the one whom God appointed as judge of the living and the dead. All the prophets testify about Him that everyone who believes in Him receives forgiveness of sins through his name.

The claim is that Christ had many appearances after his resurrection, including appearing to more than five hundred at one time. Think about this. Could five hundred people collaborate on a fake story? Does that really seem reasonable to you?

1 Corinthians 15:3-8

'For I delivered to you as of first importance what I also received, that Christ died for our sins according to the Scriptures, and that He was buried, and that He was raised on the third day according to the Scriptures, and that He appeared to Cephas, then to the twelve. After that He appeared to more than five hundred brethren at one time, most of whom remain until now,

but some have fallen asleep; then He appeared to James, then to all the apostles; and last of all, as to one untimely born, He appeared to me also. '

> **Some say the friends stole the body. But, if they stole the body, would they die for something they knew was really false and would Saul of Tarsus have changed his mind about the resurrection of Christ?**

The apostles are basing their eye witness testimony on the fact that they ate and drank with Jesus after He rose from the dead. Pretty amazing claim and remember you as a jury member have to deliberate on this issue. Are they fabricating this, or do they really believe it?

Acts 10:40-43

'God raised Him up on the third day and granted that He become visible, not to all the people, but to witnesses who were chosen beforehand by God, that is, to us who ate and drank with Him after He arose from the dead. And He ordered us to preach to the people, and solemnly to testify that this is the One who has been appointed by God as Judge of the living and the dead. Of Him all the prophets bear witness that through His name everyone who believes in Him receives forgiveness of sins." '

So, what happened to the physical body of Jesus after he had been seen by his apostles for a period of over 40 days on multiple occurrences? Here is what they said happened.

Acts 1:9-11

'After he said this, He was taken up before their very eyes, and a cloud hid Him from their sight. They were looking intently up into the sky as He was going, when suddenly two men dressed in white stood beside them. "Men of Galilee," they said, "why do you stand here looking into the sky? This same Jesus, who has been taken from you into heaven, will come back in the same way you have seen Him go into heaven." '

Remember back to the first two witnesses. Some say the friends stole the body. But, if they stole the body, would they die for something they knew was really false and would Saul of Tarsus have changed his mind about the resurrection of Christ? You have to take the full body of testimony into consideration and decide your verdict on the evidence presented and the testimony given. Remember, no jury member ever witnessed the events about which they are asked to make a decision. So what are you thinking so far? Let's call another witness for you to consider.

IV. Witness #4: The coming of the Holy Spirit on Pentecost

John 16:5-13

'"But now I am going to Him who sent Me; and none of you asks Me, 'Where are You going?' But because I have said these things to you, sorrow has filled your heart. But I tell you the truth, it is to your advantage that I go away; <u>for if I do not go away, the Helper will not come to you; but if I go, I will send Him to you</u>. And He, when He comes, will convict the world concerning sin and righteousness and judgment; concerning sin, because they do not believe in Me; and concerning righteousness, because I go to the Father and you no longer see Me; and concerning judgment, because the ruler of this world has been judged. "I have many more things to say to you, but you cannot bear them now. But when He, the Spirit of truth, comes, He will guide you into all the truth; for He will not speak on His own initiative, but whatever He hears, He will speak; and He will disclose to you what is to come. '

Jesus is talking to his disciples. What did Jesus say MUST happen BEFORE the Holy Spirit would come? He said he had to go away first, then he would send the Holy Spirit. Then we already saw the event when Jesus ascends into heaven. Let's look again.

Acts 1:1-11

'In my former book, Theophilus, I wrote about all that Jesus began to do and to teach until the day he was taken up to heaven, after giving instructions through the Holy Spirit to the apostles he had chosen. After his suffering, he presented Himself

to them and gave many convincing proofs that he was alive. He appeared to them over a period of forty days and spoke about the kingdom of God. On one occasion, while he was eating with them, he gave them this command: "<u>Do not leave Jerusalem, but wait for the gift my Father promised, which you have heard me speak about. For John baptized with water, but in a few days you will be baptized with the Holy Spirit.</u>" Then they gathered around Him and asked Him, "Lord, are you at this time going to restore the kingdom to Israel?" He said to them: "It is not for you to know the times or dates the Father has set by his own authority. But you will receive power when the Holy Spirit comes on you; and you will be my witnesses in Jerusalem, and in all Judea and Samaria, and to the ends of the earth." After he said this, he was taken up before their very eyes, and a cloud hid Him from their sight. They were looking intently up into the sky as he was going, when suddenly two men dressed in white stood beside them. "Men of Galilee," they said, "why do you stand here looking into the sky? This same Jesus, who has been taken from you into heaven, will come back in the same way you have seen Him go into heaven." '

Jesus is talking to His apostles and tells them they would receive the Holy Spirit but they had to remain in Jerusalem until He came. He ascends into heaven leaving them awestruck. Remember, this is what Jesus said must happen before the Holy Spirit would come. Now let's see what happens just a few days later.

Acts 2:1-4

'When the day of Pentecost came, they were all together in one place. Suddenly a sound like the blowing of a violent wind came from heaven and filled the whole house where they were sitting. They saw what seemed to be tongues of fire that separated and came to rest on each of them. All of them were filled with the Holy Spirit and began to speak in other tongues as the Spirit enabled them. '

So the Holy Spirit comes on the apostles with a miraculous power not seen before and everyone at Pentecost is drawn to this occurrence wondering what in the world is happening!

Peter and the other eleven are speaking fluently in other languages they never knew and the audience is amazed to hear these Galilean's speaking their own native languages fluently. Something very strange was happening.

> *Acts 2:6-12*
>
> *When they heard this sound, a crowd came together in bewilderment, because each one heard their own language being spoken. Utterly amazed, they asked: "Aren't all these who are speaking Galileans? Then how is it that each of us hears them in our native language? Parthians, Medes and Elamites; residents of Mesopotamia, Judea and Cappadocia, Pontus and Asia, Phrygia and Pamphylia, Egypt and the parts of Libya near Cyrene; visitors from Rome (both Jews and converts to Judaism); Cretans and Arabs—we hear them declaring the wonders of God in our own tongues!" Amazed and perplexed, they asked one another, "What does this mean?" '*

Peter explains that what they are seeing and hearing is evidence of what God had long ago promised through the prophet David. This is evidence that Jesus has in fact been raised from the dead as predicted by David.

> *Acts 2:31-33*
>
> *"Fellow Israelites, I can tell you confidently that the patriarch David died and was buried and his tomb is here to this day. But he was a prophet and knew that God had promised Him on oath that he would place one of his descendants on his throne. <u>Seeing what was to come, he spoke of the resurrection of the Messiah, that he was not abandoned to the realm of the dead, nor did his body see decay. God has raised this Jesus to life, and we are all witnesses of it. Exalted to the right hand of God, he has received</u>*

from the Father the promised Holy Spirit and has poured out
what you now see and hear. '

Peter acknowledges that God promised through David a thousand years earlier that he would raise one of his descendants, Jesus, and exalt Him to his own right hand. The astounding prediction is that he would not be abandoned to the realm of the dead and his body would not decay. No one really understood what that meant until today.

Peter concludes by saying that everything that was predicted in the Old Testament, their own eye-witness testimony that they ate and drank with Jesus after his resurrection and the miraculous coming of the Holy Spirit all collaborate to the truthfulness that Jesus has been raised from the dead, and is in fact the promised Messiah and all the claims about Him are verified beyond a reasonable doubt.

Acts 2:36-41

Therefore let all Israel be assured of this: God has made this Jesus, whom you crucified, both Lord and Messiah." When the people heard this, they were cut to the heart and said to Peter and the other apostles, "Brothers, what shall we do?" Peter replied, "Repent and be baptized, every one of you, in the name of Jesus Christ for the forgiveness of your sins. And you will receive the gift of the Holy Spirit. The promise is for you and your children and for all who are far off—for all whom the Lord our God will call." With many other words he warned them; and he pleaded with them, "Save yourselves from this corrupt generation." Those who accepted his message were baptized, and about three thousand were added to their number that day.

When the crowd saw the power of the Holy Spirit coming upon the apostles and empowered them to speak foreign languages they never before knew, they were convinced something in history had changed. Peter preached Old Testament scriptures they heard in Synagogue as kids and perhaps had discussions on what they meant – one of David's descendants sitting on his throne, his body not decaying, and David calling one of his great great great grandkids his own Lord? What's that all about? As the king, you never call one of your descendants your own

Lord, but David said his Lord would be one of his descendants. Peter concludes his argument, "Therefore, God has made this Jesus whom you crucified both Lord and Christ."

This message cut many to their hearts and they wanted to know how in the world they could ever make this right with God. You might be asking the same question. How can you make what you've done in your life right with God? What comes to mind? Perhaps you wince when you think of something you wish you'd never done; An affair or the look that caused you to lust; An abortion; A divorce; A bad relationship with your parents; An addiction? The lie you remember telling or the income you never reported on your taxes? What cuts you to the heart? Are you asking the same question they asked on Pentecost? "What shall I do? What can I do to pay for what I've done?" The answer is – NOTHING! You can never "undo" what you've done. A penalty is required; a payment must be extracted.

If killing God's Son is forgivable, then you can pretty much hang your hat on the guarantee that your sins can be forgiven no matter how horrible you think they are. But, remember that this free gift of forgiveness is still

Not one of us is innocent. We've all sinned and the penalty for just a single sin is capital punishment – death. We can't undo what we've done. The punishment must be extracted. You can pay for it yourself, or you can accept Christ's payment for your sin. Easy choice! It's free but it does have some conditions.

conditional. But it's the day of Pentecost, remember? The Israelites in Egypt had to have the blood of the lamb on their door so that judgment would "Passover" them. And we have to have the blood of the Lamb of God covering us if God's judgment is going to pass over us. The Bible claims that Jesus took the electric chair – the cross in our place. His blood will cause judgment to pass over us, but we still have to apply the blood.

Did you see what Peter told them to do? Read it again. "Repent (change your thinking, turn around) and be baptized (immersed, buried in water) for the forgiveness of your sins and you will receive the gift of the Holy Spirit." He kept on pleading and begging them to meet the conditions of the terms of this free pardon, *'And with many other words he solemnly testified and kept on exhorting them, saying 'Be saved.' So those who accepted his message were baptized, and there were added about three thousand souls."* (Acts 2:40-41). We'll talk about this a lot more in a later chapter, but did you notice what Peter did NOT say? He didn't ask the crowd to make an "alter call" or say a "sinner's prayer" or "invite Jesus into their hearts." He told them to repent and be baptized, every one of them in the name of Jesus Christ for the forgiveness of their sins.

Three thousand responded when Peter told them to save themselves- and were baptized the first day the church began because of something they heard, saw and understood. What if you'd been there? Well, you're kind of there now that you have to make some decision about what you hear.

As a jury member ask yourself this question. Do you think three thousand people could have heard and seen something that was not there? Not likely! Three thousand people saw and heard the exact same thing then they were baptized because of the reasoning that Jesus was raised from the dead. David promised it a thousand years earlier and these average Galilean fishermen were speaking fluent foreign languages they never before learned and testifying that that they ate and drank with Jesus after he rose from the dead and He promised that He'd send the Holy Spirit which the crowd now saw and heard.

You're in the deliberation room of your life. Remember, no jury was ever a witness to the events presented in court. They must base their decision on the testimony presented. The verdict you decide doesn't affect some unknown defendant; it affects you and your eternity. So, what's your verdict - true or false?

V. Conclusion:
The evidence for the resurrection of Christ is strong and logical. The disciples of Jesus were changed in a very short time and were willing to

die for their claim that they ate and drank with Jesus after he rose from the dead.

Saul of Tarsus, a persecutor of the Christian message, was changed rapidly and was willing to forfeit his inheritance as a Jew, his freedom, and even his life for the claim that he saw Jesus after the resurrection. He changed rapidly and became the greatest advocate of the resurrection of Jesus in history.

The Jews, who do not believe in the resurrection of Christ to this very day, have yet to produce a simple dead corpse to discredit the resurrection claim. They have no evidence or proof that it didn't happen!

The Holy Spirit's appearance on Pentecost was evidence enough for over three thousand Jews to be convinced of the resurrection of Christ. Be real here. Something happened!

Here's the most important question of your life that only you can answer. Do you believe that Jesus of Nazareth rose from the dead as recorded in the Bible? That's a question that only you can answer. You're the jury member, you've heard the testimony and now you must decide - true or false? At this point I've never had a single person tell me they didn't believe in the resurrection of Jesus. If I'm honest with myself, I can't begin to deny it based on the evidence presented. How about you?

If you do believe that Jesus did in fact rise from the dead, then here are the implications.

1. Jesus is the divine Son of God. All the claims that the Bible make about Him are true. He is God in the flesh, He's eternal, He's the creator of the universe, He has ultimate authority over the physical and spiritual world and He will be the judge of the entire world including Buddha and Mohammed, you and me.

2. Sin is a reality and we have all sinned and fallen short of the perfection that is required to be saved. Unless we believe in Jesus and His plan of salvation, we will die in our sins and be lost for all eternity and be cast into the lake of fire along with the devil and his angels. We either accept His payment for our sins, or we pay ourselves. God's a gentleman and will not force Himself on you. The choice it totally yours.

   John 8:24

   'I told you that you would die in your sins; if you do not believe that I am he, you will indeed die in your sins." '

3. There is a judgment day coming and Jesus will be the judge.

   John 12:48

   'There is a judge for the one who rejects me and does not accept my words; the very words I have spoken will condemn them at the last day. '

4. We must all stand before the judgment seat of Christ and give account. Either we pay for our own sins, which is impossible, or we accept His free gift and can be pardoned and deemed innocent and made "Just as if we had never sinned."

   2 Corinthians 5:10

   'For we must all appear before the judgment seat of Christ, so that each of us may receive what is due us for the things done while in the body, whether good or bad. '

5. The Bible is true because Jesus confirmed the Old Testament as true.

   Luke 24:44-47

   'He said to them, "This is what I told you while I was still with you: Everything must be fulfilled that is written about me in the Law of Moses, the Prophets and the Psalms." Then he opened their minds so they could understand the Scriptures. He told them, "This is what is written: The Messiah will suffer and rise from the dead on the third day, and repentance for the

forgiveness of sins will be preached in his name to all nations, beginning at Jerusalem. '

6. The Bible is true because Jesus authored the New Testament and it is his Last Will and Testament and we are the beneficiaries when we meet the conditions in the will.

    Hebrews 9:15

    'For this reason Christ is the mediator of a new covenant, that those who are called may receive the promised eternal inheritance—now that he has died as a ransom to set them free from the sins committed under the first covenant. '

7. Christianity is the one and only religion acceptable to God. I know that might sound a bit arrogant, but it's really not. If Jesus was raised from the dead, then He alone is God and no one else is. This is a very narrow statement and not well-accepted in our politically correct culture where we don't want to offend anyone. Forget all that. If Jesus is who He says it is and is raised from the dead, then He's the only one who can defend you and pay your penalty on the Day of Judgment.

    John 14:6

    I am the way, the truth and the life. No one comes to the father except by me.

    Acts 4:12

    'Salvation is found in no one else, for there is <u>no other name under heaven given to mankind by which we must be saved."</u> '

Well, there you have it. Who is Jesus? Is there reasonable and substantial evidence based on credible testimony that makes sense? I think there is, but what about you?

I hope you're grasping the magnitude of what you're reading up to this point. God became a man because He loves us. God in human flesh allowed Himself to be tortured and killed to pay for the sins that you and the entire human race have committed because He loves us that much. Hard to believe that kind of love isn't it? To verify this He was raised from the dead after three days in a cold dark tomb. Do you believe this? You're on the jury and you must make a decision - true or false. It affects the credibility of the Christian message, but more importantly, it affects your eternity. Remember the beginning of the book? You'll be alive one billion years from now; the question is where? Are you really considering this evidence and the claims? Don't believe just because you were born into a Christian nation or family. Don't be swayed into believing something experiential just because there's some feeling or tradition that feels good to you. Believe only because your heart and your mind can trust the evidence. Faith is the EVIDENCE of things not seen. You've heard the evidence of things you haven't seen yourself just like those in a jury.

If you believe Jesus has been raised from the dead and the claims about Him in Chapter one, welcome! We're going into deeper examination about how to become a follower of Jesus and how do you get in on this amazing deal! To do this, you must understand the love letter God gave to us – The Bible. Let's look at how to understand it and the message that applies to your life!

Ready to dive in? Great, let's go!

Chapter 4 - The Word of God

 Many people are unfamiliar with how the Bible is organized and how to read it properly. I was like that when I first starting trying to read it when I was twenty years old. I didn't understand "who begat whom" and what about those weird ceremonies about burnt offerings and new moon celebrations and some of the other stuff in the Bible. How does that apply to me; or does it?

I've since written an entire course on "Introduction to the Bible" (www.gregbiblestudy.blogspot.com) which helps you understand the Bible chronologically. But for now, let's just focus on the basics so you'll have a good starting place. Sound like a deal?

Let's talk about the difference between the Old and New Testament in your Bible. There are two major sections in your Bible, the Old and New Testament. So let's first talk about what covenant or testament are we under today and why. There are basically three covenant periods in the Bible.

First is the covenant God made with Abraham, the father of the Jewish people. In this covenant, God promised that through his "seed" all the nations of the earth would be blessed. That seed promise was fulfilled in Jesus but continues as a promise for those who are clothed in Christ and become heirs of the covenant promise made to Abraham, *"And if you belong to Christ, then you are Abraham's descendants, heirs according to promise," (Galatians 3:29).*

Second is the covenant God made with Israel which included the Ten Commandment law and the over 613 subsequent laws, regulations and practices. And finally, the third is the New Covenant which God made through Jesus.

In this chapter we will examine very briefly how God gave us the Bible, what testament applies to us today, and what attitudes are necessary in order to be pleasing to God as we read the Bible. I think you're going to be a bit surprised at what you're about to learn. Keep reading and take notes and underline stuff that you read. This book is for you!

I. Which Testament Are We under Today

> John 1:17

> *For the law was given through Moses; grace and truth came through Jesus Christ.*

From this verse I want you to notice a few things. **The Law of Moses** – referring to the Old Testament, specifically the first five books of the Bible came through Moses. This is where you'll find the Ten Commandments, but there are actually a total of 613 laws contained in the Law of Moses. Don't worry about that; just understand there is something drastically different between what Moses gave us and what Jesus instituted.

> **It always amuses me when people say, "I keep the ten commandments" thinking they're OK with God. Most don't even know the Ten Commandments let alone knowing that they will kill them for eternity if they break just one of them in their entire life!**

Grace and truth came through Jesus Christ. The books of Romans and Galatians in the New Testament go into great detail explaining this difference between law and grace, but suffice it to say that Jesus brought in a system of grace and truth, literally *grace-truth* in the Greek.

So what's different between the Law of Moses and the New Covenant of Jesus? Let's look at some passages and find out.

> Acts 13:38-39

> *Therefore, my friends, I want you to know that through Jesus the forgiveness of sins is proclaimed to you. <u>Through Him</u> everyone*

*who believes is set free from every sin, a justification **you were not able to obtain under the Law of Moses.***

OK, now pay careful attention to what has just been said in this verse. Through Jesus the forgiveness of sins is made available and we are set free from sin and its' penalty. This is what's called *justification* which means "Just as if I'd" never sinned. It's a legal status that we already talked about earlier. This legal status of being pardoned and deemed innocent was not available under the Law of Moses. The Law told you what the rules were, and then condemned you because it was impossible to keep it perfectly your whole life without breaking it even one single time. The Law showed you what sin was, but never offered pardon once you broke it. It was a horrible burden. Talk about a guilt-trip!

So the natural question arises, "Was the Law a mistake or was it *sinful* by being so "unforgiving?"" The answer is no. Look at these verses.

Romans 7:7 -12

> *What shall we say, then? Is the law sinful? Certainly not! Nevertheless, I would not have known what sin was had it not been for the law. For I would not have known what coveting really was if the law had not said, "You shall not covet." But sin, seizing the opportunity afforded by the commandment, produced in me every kind of coveting. For apart from the law, sin was dead. I found that the very commandment that was intended to bring life actually brought death. For sin, seizing the opportunity afforded by the commandment, deceived me, and through the commandment put me to death. So then, the law is holy, and the commandment is holy, righteous and good.*

Here we have the Apostle Paul (Saul of Tarsus who saw Jesus on the road to Damascus) giving a discourse explaining the function and purpose of the Law of Moses and even quotes the tenth of the Ten Commandments – *Thou Shalt Not Covet.* Have you ever seen a sign, "Wet paint; do not touch?" When you read that sign what did you want to do? Exactly, you wanted to touch the paint. That's how we're wired. Speed limit 65 mph; so you go 67 just to go over the limit; but not far enough to get a ticket. I know how you think; me too! We always push the limit of a law just because we don't like someone or something telling us what we can't or shouldn't do. When you see "Don't Touch" you want to touch. You would have never thought about it had you not seen the sign.

That's how law works. That's how rule keeping plays with our mind and makes us do the very thing we're told *NOT to do*. So the law created in us the desire to do that which was forbidden and when we did it, it turned around and killed us, and didn't offer a solution. *"Sin seized the opportunity afforded by the commandment, deceived me, and through the commandment put me to death."* The Law is perfect, but we're not and that's the point Paul is making. So there has to be another solution, right?

> *Romans 8:1-4*
>
> *Therefore, there is now no condemnation for those who are in Christ Jesus, because through Christ Jesus <u>the law of the Spirit who gives life has set you free from the law of sin and death</u>. <u>For what the law was powerless to do because it was weakened by the flesh, God did by sending his own Son in the likeness of sinful flesh</u> to be a sin offering. And so he condemned sin in the flesh, in order that the righteous requirement of the law might be fully met in us, who do not live according to the flesh but according to the Spirit.* '

The law condemned, but now through the New Covenant in Christ, there is no condemnation once we meet His terms of pardon offered by grace. There's a difference between Spirit and Flesh. The New Covenant, the law of the Spirit, sets us free from the law of sin and death – The Law of Moses and any kind of law system. Jesus condemned sin in the flesh in order that the righteous requirements of the Law of Moses might be fully met. He paid the penalty demanded by the Law on the cross when "God made Him who knew no sin to be sin for us" and in return we become the righteousness of God "In Him." We'll talk more about that later. Just understand there is sharp contrast between Law given through Moses and grace-truth that is offered through Jesus.

You've heard of a person's Last Will and Testament. A testament is legal contract that goes into force when the person who made it (the testator) dies. While he's still alive, it can be changed and altered, but when he dies, all other and previous testaments are annulled and the last will of the Testator now becomes the legal document. We'll see that the New Testament is Jesus' "last will and testament" and it went into force the second he died on the cross. Until that moment the Old Testament Law of Moses was in force. Let's look at some verses that explain this.

You must remember this important point for later on. Jesus' Last will and Testament (New Testament) went into force the second he died, not before. You'll understand why later! Don't forget this!

> Hebrews 9:15-17
>
> *'For this reason Christ is the mediator of a new covenant, that those who are called may receive the promised eternal inheritance—now that he has died as a ransom to set them free from the sins committed under the first covenant. In the case of a will, it is necessary to prove the death of the one who made it, because a will is in force only when somebody has died; it never takes effect while the one who made it is living. '*

So we see that Jesus is the mediator of a new covenant or testament that offers eternal inheritance since He died to set people free from the sins committed under the first (Old) covenant. His testament went into force the second he died on the cross. At that second something else happened simultaneously – the Old Testament law ceased entirely. You can't have two wills or testaments in force at the same time. That's why every last will and testament includes the clause, *"I revoke all prior wills and codicils."* That clause becomes legally binding at the second the Testator takes his last breath and his heart stops.

Hebrews 10:9

Then he said, "Here I am, I have come to do your will." He sets aside the first to establish the second.

Not only did Jesus replace the Old with the New, but the New is a much better covenant with superior promises for us as the beneficiaries of His will.

Hebrews 8:6-7

But in fact the ministry Jesus has received is as superior to theirs as <u>the covenant of which he is mediator is superior to the old one, since the new covenant is established on better promises.</u> For if there had been nothing wrong with that first covenant, no place would have been sought for another. But God found fault with the people...

So what's the problem with the former covenant? Well very simply, no one could keep it and it condemned everyone to death who violated a single law. Oh, the law was wonderful and holy and perfect. The problem is that we aren't!

Have you ever heard someone say, "Oh, I'm OK with God because I keep the Ten Commandments?" Really? Well, if you can keep them perfectly without violating one law your entire life, you're only the second person in human history that could do that. The first person to do it was Jesus Christ! The Law slaps you in the face and rubs your nose in the reality that you are a horrible sinner and "No, you can't be perfect, you can't be holy and the only way to please God is to perfectly keep the law your entire life." GUILTY! CONDEMNED! If you fail in one law, you're guilty of all 613 of them, and each carries the penalty of capital punishment for a violation! You OK with that? Not me! I need help!

Someone said the theme of the Old Testament is "Someone is Coming." Since Adam and Eve sinned in the garden, there was an immediate promise that someone would come to crush under his heel the serpent's head. Abraham was promised that through one of his descendants the nations would be blessed. The coming of Christ was promised all through the Old Testament. So what was the purpose of the Law of Moses?

Galatians 3:19-25

*Why, then, was the law given at all? It was added because of transgressions **until** <u>the Seed to whom the promise referred had come.</u> The law was given through angels and entrusted to a mediator. A mediator, however, implies more than one party; but God is one. Is the law, therefore, opposed to the promises of God? Absolutely not! <u>For if a law had been given that could impart life, then righteousness would certainly have come by the law</u>. But Scripture has locked up everything under the control of sin, so that what was promised, being given through faith in Jesus Christ, might be given to those who believe. Before the coming of this faith, we were held in custody under the law, locked up until the faith that was to come would be revealed. So the law was our guardian until Christ came that we might be justified by faith. Now that this faith has come, we are no longer under a guardian.*

WOW, the implications and statements in these verses are mind-blowing! Why was the law given at all? Great question; right? It was added because of sin; to make sin recognizable for what it really is, ugly, unholy, horrible, and deadly! But it was given UNTIL. That means it had a time-limit until the seed of Abraham to whom the promise referred in Genesis 12 had come.

Now catch this in this section. If a law could have been given that could give life, then righteousness would have come through the law. But the law doesn't care if you can keep it perfectly or not. It simply shows you that you can't! It's rigid, unforgiving, and keeps you locked up in rules, duty, effort that you can never attain. You sin – you die. But, there is a promise that while you are held in custody under the law and locked up as it were, it shows you a glimmer of hope that there is a different system coming. There's hope and it's a system of grace-truth that will be revealed through the coming seed promise of Abraham in Genesis 12. He will be the seed of the woman in Genesis 3 in the Garden of Eden who will crush the serpents' head and kill Him, but in the process His own heel will be severely bruised.

When the system of grace-truth which is obtained by faith in Jesus Christ came, we were released from the tyrannical guardian of the law. Jesus said it this way to a multitude of Jewish people who were under the law in His Sermon on the Mount

> *Matthew 11:28-30*
>
> *"Come to me, all you who are weary and burdened, and I will give you rest. Take my yoke upon you and learn from me, for I am gentle and humble in heart, and you will find rest for your souls. For my yoke is easy and my burden is light."'*

 So I want you to understand that the Law of Moses was good, perfect, holy and righteous. It was supremely good! The problem is that it demanded perfection from those under its' jurisdiction and no one could comply.

Those that tried were weary, burdened, condemned and could never have a clear conscience in their worship. If you are under this law, you're burdened with guilt and shame knowing that you could never be good enough to please God.

The law was given through Moses – a perfect law- a law that, if followed, would create a perfect humanity, perfect communities. No murder, no adultery, no lying, no wanting your neighbor's stuff or wife, no stealing and a perfect world. Sound possible? Not in this life and not in this flesh.

So Christ came and gave us grace-truth. He knew how messed up we are and would continue to be and since the law condemned those who violated the perfect law; He stepped up and kept the law perfectly, then took the condemnation demanded by the law for all those who couldn't. As God in the flesh, He took the blunt force condemnation for the entire human race so that the law and God's justice could be perfectly met, while at the same time offering forgiveness because the penalty had been paid in full by God Himself. God could then be proven "just" because He dealt with sin and issued the penalty it deserved. He was also the "justifier" of people who were guilty because the penalty had been met in the death of Jesus on the cross. God didn't sweep sin under the table at all! Never think that. *"He made Him who knew no sin to be sin for us so that we might become the righteous of God in Him!"* (2 Corinthians 5:21).

Now let's look at the New Testament and see what Jesus says about how He received it from his Father.

II. The New Testament of Jesus Christ

Matthew 7:28-29

When Jesus had finished saying these things, the crowds were amazed at his teaching, because he taught as one who had authority, and not as their teachers of the law.

Jesus' most notable sermon is what is known as The Sermon on the Mount. Throughout history it's been one of the most quoted and referenced speeches by any man at any time. It's powerful in-your-face and confrontational and at the same time tender. The sermon has three sections – Kingdom Attitudes, Kingdom Righteousness and Kingdom Entry. The crowds were amazed at his teaching because He taught as one who had authority instead of vicariously assuming authority from a teacher above you or whom you quoted. Jesus became flesh to live as a man; a God-man, but He subjected Himself to God the Father from whom He received His authority as a man in the flesh.

John 8:28

So Jesus said, "When you have lifted up the Son of Man, then you will know that I am he and that I do nothing on my own but speak just what the Father has taught me.

God wanted to verify that Jesus' message was confirmed by Him. Jesus ascends on a mountain with Peter, James and John and miraculously meets in a cloud with Moses and Elijah who had been dead for more than a thousand years. Then Peter, James and John witness an unbelievable event. Put yourself in their place. What would you think and feel about this? God Himself speaks from heaven with this proclamation:

Matthew 17:5

While he was still speaking, a bright cloud covered them, and a voice from the cloud said, "This is my Son, whom I love; with Him I am well pleased. Listen to Him!" When the disciples heard this, they fell facedown to the ground, terrified.

I know I would be terrified as well and like the disciples, I'd fall facedown in absolute fear. Wouldn't you? God the Father was well pleased with what Jesus was teaching and His authority was from the throne of heaven itself. Don't listen to Moses or Elijah. Jesus now has all authority.

Matthew 28:18

Then Jesus came to them and said, "All authority in heaven and on earth has been given to me."

Now think about this. If Jesus as all authority not only on earth, but in heaven, is there any authority that He doesn't have? Nope. All means "all". Remember back to the claims of Jesus in chapter one where He has all authority over the demons and even the physical elements to calm the sea? God gave all authority to Jesus and that's how God speaks to the human race in these days – through His Son and to us as beneficiaries of His last will and testament.

In the Old Testament, God used to speak to different people at different times and in different ways. He spoke to Moses in a burning bush and on top of Mount Sinai in a cloud of smoke and fire. He spoke to Jacob and Daniel in dreams. But in these days He speaks to us through Jesus and His testament. Remember, Jesus is the heir of the universe and in fact, through Him the universe was created! Think you might want to listen to what he has to say? I do.

> Hebrews 1:1-2
>
> *In the past God spoke to our ancestors through the prophets at many times and in various ways, but in these last days he has spoken to us by his Son, whom he appointed heir of all things, and through whom also he made the universe.*

So, if Jesus received his authority from the Father and He has total authority, who do you think you'll be accountable to at the judgment day? You and I will be held accountable to Jesus and His words and our faith in His promise to offer us forgiveness of sins and take upon Himself our sins.

> John 12:48-50
>
> *There is a judge for the one who rejects me and does not accept my words; the very words I have spoken will condemn them at the last day. "If anyone hears my words but does not keep them, I do not judge that person. For I did not come to judge (Condemn) the world, but to save the world. For I did not speak on my own, but the Father who sent me commanded me to say all that I have spoken. I know that his command leads to eternal life. So whatever I say is just what the Father has told me to say."*[1]

Jesus' words and His New Covenant will be the standard of judgment on the last day. You're going to be excited to see what the court room of heaven looks like when we get there in a later chapter. Stay tuned and keep reading! That's why it's called "Good News!"

Jesus is the mediator of a new covenant that went into force the second He died. Then He has to ensure that His beneficiaries get the benefits and information bequeathed to them. So, Jesus transmits His message to the spokesmen who will fill the earth with this message – His apostles. Just before His trial, Jesus prays to His father and reassures Him that the message and testament He'd been entrusted with has been faithfully transmitted to those who would carry the news to the world.

John 17:7,8,14,17

I have revealed you to those whom you gave me out of the world. They were yours; you gave them to me and they have obeyed your word. Now they know that everything you have given me comes from you. For I gave them the words you gave me and they accepted them. They knew with certainty that I came from you, and they believed that you sent me.

I have given them your word and the world has hated them, for they are not of the world any more than I am of the world. Sanctify them by the truth; your word is truth. As you sent me into the world, I have sent them into the world.

On every last will and testament, you have to have a Notary to verify that your signature is legitimate and that your testament is in fact what you desire to be implemented. The New Testament of Jesus is no different. There isn't an office with a stamp or seal to notarize His last will. There's something better - legitimate, verifiable miracles. I'm not talking about the ones you might see by some counterfeit miracle worker who slap people on the head and they fall on the floor because they are subject to hypnotism or suggestion. How about a guy that's been dead four days and you take him to lunch? How about a guy who has never walked his whole life and on main street every day begging for money for a burger, and now he's dancing in town square with the people who used to drop a few coins in his cup? Or how about a guy who has been blind his whole life and the whole town now sees the guy reading a news paper at the coffee shop?

Mark 16:20

Then the disciples went out and preached everywhere, and the Lord worked with them and <u>confirmed his word by the signs that accompanied it.</u>

Once a document has been notarized, do you think it has to be notarized every time it's read? Are you kidding me? Once a document is verifiably legitimate you don't have to verify it every time it's read. That's the argument of Jude who urges that followers of Christ must contend, argue, urge, and defend this faith that was one time for all time delivered and doesn't need reconfirmation.

Jude 3

Dear friends, although I was very eager to write to you about the salvation we share, I felt compelled to write and urge you to contend for <u>the faith that was once for all entrusted to God's holy people.</u>

So, God gave His word to Jesus who made His last will and notarized it with miraculous confirmation. Now He has to continue getting the message to those who will write it down and pass it along accurately and understandably to the entire list of beneficiaries – the world!

Ephesians 3:1-6

For this reason I, Paul, the prisoner of Christ Jesus for the sake of you Gentiles— Surely you have heard about <u>the administration of God's grace that was given to me for you,</u> In <u>reading this, then, you will be able to understand my insight into the mystery of Christ,</u> This mystery is that through the gospel the Gentiles are heirs together with Israel, members together of one body, and sharers together in the promise in Christ Jesus. which was not made known to people in other generations as it has now been revealed by the Spirit to God's holy apostles and prophets; that is, the mystery made known to me by revelation, as <u>I have already written briefly.</u> '

These administrators are like executors of a will and did not have the authority or permission to change or alter the last will and testament of the testator. They couldn't add their own interpretation into the legal document. When the testator died, they were the administrators and their duty was to write what the testator told them to write without any intervention or biased alteration from them. These men were carried along and guided by the Holy Spirit to ensure accurate transmission. Many of the prophets of the Old Testament did not comprehend what they were even writing about, but they wrote faithfully the exact message. For instance, Isaiah wrote about Christ's death 600 years before it happened as he was inspired by the Holy Spirit. No questions; just write. Sounds like a news report from a past event; but this example is 600 years before it happened!

Isaiah 53:1-12

'Who has believed our message and to whom has the arm of the Lord been revealed? He was despised and rejected by mankind, a man of suffering, and familiar with pain. Like one from whom people hide their faces he was despised, and we held Him in low esteem. Surely he took up our pain and bore our suffering, yet we considered Him punished by God, stricken by Him, and afflicted. But he was pierced for our transgressions, he was crushed for our iniquities; the punishment that brought us peace was on Him, and by his wounds we are healed. We all, like sheep, have gone astray, each of us has turned to our own way; and the Lord has laid on Him the iniquity of us all. He was oppressed and afflicted, yet he did not open his mouth; he was led like a lamb to the slaughter, and as a sheep before its shearers is silent, so he did not open his mouth. By oppression and judgment he was taken away. Yet who of his generation protested? For he was cut off from the land of the living; for the transgression of my people he was punished. He was assigned a grave with the wicked and with the rich in his death, though he had done no violence, nor was any deceit in his mouth. Yet it was the Lord's will to crush Him and cause Him to suffer, and though the Lord makes his life an offering for sin, he will see his offspring and prolong his days, and the will of the Lord will prosper in his hand. After he has suffered, he will see the light of life and be satisfied; by his knowledge my righteous servant will justify many, and he will

bear their iniquities. Therefore I will give Him a portion among the great, and he will divide the spoils with the strong, because he poured out his life unto death, and was numbered with the transgressors. For he bore the sin of many, and made intercession for the transgressors.'

David wrote about one of his descendants sitting upon his throne who he would submit to as his own Lord. Unthinkable, but he just wrote. Administrators write what is given them; nothing more. God gave the word to Jesus who gave it to his apostles as administrators and they wrote it down. When we read it we can understand clearly our part as beneficiaries of Jesus' last will and testament.

2 Peter 1:20-21

Above all, you must understand that no prophecy of Scripture came about by the prophet's own interpretation. For prophecy never had its origin in the human will, but prophets, though human, spoke from God as they were carried along by the Holy Spirit.

Here's what these verses teach in a nutshell. God gave the word to Jesus, who gave it to the apostles and verified it by miraculous confirmation and thus notarized the will. The apostles were administrators of God's grace-truth last will and testament of Jesus that was given to the world through the apostles. They wrote everything down by guidance and direction of the Holy Spirit to ensure it was totally accurate and that no human interference or interpretation could alter the will of the testator. When I, as a beneficiary, read what these administrators wrote down about God's grace and Jesus Last Will and Testament I should understand clearly what I have coming to me – right?

I should also understand my responsibility as a conditional recipient of this free gift given to me by the Testator of the will. After all, His death made all this possible for me as a recipient, right? So, if I want to be a beneficiary and receive my inheritance, it would be a wise thing to understand the will and follow the requirements of the parameters of the testator. I didn't do anything to be a beneficiary. I didn't buy my way into the will. I'm simply a gracious recipient of the testator, but there are conditions in the will. Free, but still conditional. Let's look at that a little bit more.

Have you heard about families torn apart when someone dies and the kids all fight over the will? The second oldest son makes up some story about a conversation he had with his dad in the boat and contests the will or tries to alter something in the written will. Happens all the time, right? There's nothing new here. People throughout history have attempted to change, alter and distort the will to get more for themselves or deny the lawful beneficiaries their inheritance.

> *2 Peter 3:15-17*
>
> *Bear in mind that our Lord's patience means salvation, just as our dear brother <u>Paul also wrote you </u>with the wisdom that God gave Him. He writes the same way in all his letters, speaking in them of these matters. His letters contain some things that are hard to understand, which <u>ignorant and unstable people distort, as they do the other Scriptures, to their own destruction. Therefore, dear friends, since you have been forewarned, be on your guard so that you may not be carried away by the error of the lawless and fall from your secure position.</u>*

Jealous relatives, envious neighbors and even uninformed friends can think a will is unfair and will try to change it. The first time I witnessed this was when I was 14 years old working in the Floral Park Nursery. It was a green house where my aunt Gladys worked and she got me hired on. I rode my bike to work about a mile away every day after school and on the weekends my step dad Pat would drive me to work. It paid $1.25 an hour and in those days for a 14 year old kid that was minimum wage and I was banking some cash. Meryl was the owner of the green house and a really nice guy. He was mid 40's, slim and drove a white and red trimmed 69 Ford half-ton pickup.

A couple of years earlier I was going to visit my dad in Las Vegas and flew for my first time. I told Meryl my story and he responded with this statement, "I'd never get on an airplane! Those things will kill you." At that I retorted with my best come-back. "Well Meryl, when it's your time to go, it your time to go!" He responded, "Well, what if I'm up there with you and it's you're time to go?"I questioned if I should jump on an airplane and visit my dad! What if I'm up there and it's someone else's time to go and he was right? Meryl had a heart attack a month later in his green house at forty five years old and died, but he never rode on an air plane. I flew to spend time with my dad, but Meryl could have robbed me of that adventure had I listened to his reasoning. Nice guy, but dead wrong! Sometimes well-meaning people rob you of your blessing, and that happens in religion also.

When you read the New Testament, you'll see a lot of "well meaning" very religious people who try to change the grace of God into a system of religion. They want to impose rules, rituals and practices that Jesus' last will never included. Catch this! Jesus was actually killed because He wasn't religious enough and He hung around the wrong kind of people. Can you believe that? Are you kidding me? Don't let people do this to you. Here's what God says about people who try to bind religion on you instead of the grace of Christ.

> Galatians 1:6-9
>
> '*I am astonished that you are so quickly deserting the one who called you to live in the <u>grace of Christ</u> and are turning to a different gospel— which is really no gospel at all. Evidently some people are throwing you into confusion and are trying to pervert the gospel of Christ. But even if we or an angel from heaven should preach a gospel other than the one we preached to you, let them be under God's curse! As we have already said, so now I say again: If anybody is preaching to you a gospel other than what you accepted, let them be under God's curse! '*

The Greek says "Let them be **anathema"** let them be accursed! He says that twice! So if someone is telling you to try to be saved with good works or doing penance or by keeping man-made rules or by submitting to the Old Testament, including the Ten Commandments, then they and you could be accursed. Don't substitute law for grace-truth which Jesus introduced. It feels so good to try to be good and do good stuff to make God like you and let you into heaven! But that thinking will send you the other way. You can't earn your way to heaven and anyone who attempts to do that has fallen away from grace (Galatians 5:4).

God doesn't take lightly those who change or alter His word. Those who change grace to law are accursed. Look at another section that warns against changing God's word.

> Revelation 22:18-19
>
> *I warn everyone who hears the words of the prophecy of this scroll: If anyone adds anything to them, God will add to that person the plagues described in this scroll. And if anyone takes words away from this scroll of prophecy, God will take away from that person any share in the tree of life and in the Holy City, which are described in this scroll.*

There are a lot of "Christian" religions that add all their own stuff to the grace of Christ. "Don't do this, dress this way, speak this way." Some have "clergy" who step up as your mediators over you or between you and God to offer you atonement if you say this many prayers and do penance or light this candle or say this Novena. Paul through the Holy Spirit warns severely that those who do that are accursed and those who add or take away from the simple grace of Christ won't be in the Holy City of heaven. This is some serious stuff and I hope you're paying attention. It's not about religion; it's about an honest, simple relationship with your Creator through His Son and the only mediator - Jesus Christ. Just you and Him! Don't let religion or authorities or rules get in your way.

III. Our Attitude toward the Word of God

Have you ever had someone tell you something true about yourself that you might not particularly like? You know it's true, but pride makes you angry and your mouth kicks in and you start to defend or justify yourself. We've all done it at one time or another. Well, when you hear or read the word of God the same thing can happen. It's brutally honest and will show you things about yourself or your beliefs that you might not particularly like. How should you react? Let's take a look.

James 1:19-25

'*My dear brothers and sisters, take note of this: Everyone should be quick to listen, slow to speak and slow to become angry, because human anger does not produce the righteousness that God desires. Therefore, get rid of all moral filth and the evil that is so prevalent and* <u>*humbly accept the word planted in you, which can save you.*</u> *Do not merely listen to the word, and so deceive yourselves. Do what it says. Anyone who listens to the word but does not do what it says is like someone who looks at his face in a mirror and, after looking at Himself, goes away and immediately forgets what he looks like. But whoever looks intently into the perfect law that gives freedom, and continues in it—not forgetting what they have heard, but doing it—they will be blessed in what they do.* '

James is encouraging us to have the correct attitude when we hear or read God's word. We should be quick to listen to it, not resistant. We should be slow to speak against it because deep down, you know it's true! Don't justify your beliefs or actions, just eagerly listen! Don't get angry. Just humbly accept the word that you hear. Why? Because it can save you! Pay attention. God doesn't want you to perish and be cast into the lake of fire. "God is not willing for any to perish, but for all to come to repentance!" He loves you dearly and needs to speak to you truthfully. Are you listening? Really listening?

Do you have a few pounds that you'd like to lose or do you know someone who does? I bet you could tell me without thinking about it what you need to do to lose weight, right? Eat healthy, get more exercise. It's pretty simple, but as someone who needs to lose some weight myself, I know what to do, I just don't do it. I can't explain why I don't, but I just don't.

James doesn't want us to have that attitude when it comes to being saved. Don't just listen to the word of God and say, "Man, that was a good sermon," then walk away and don't put into practice what you just heard. The person who hears the word, then walks away and doesn't do it is like a man who looks in the mirror and sees his hair all messed up and his eyes all crusty, but doesn't do anything about it. When he walks away from the mirror, he forgets what he looks like and nothing changes. He's still a mess.

The word will show you what you really look like, and sometimes it's pretty frightening. You don't look so good. You have a choice. Fix up the mess you're looking at, or walk away and forget what you just looked at and deceive yourself that you're a good looking stud! God and everyone else can see you aren't because you didn't clean yourself up. But, if you fix up the mess that you see you will be blessed. Just remember that at times you're not going to initially like what you see, but its God being real with you and showing you what you really look like through His word. His intention is to make you look like Christ and have His character!

He's giving you everything – a new life – eternal life. But you must know the truth in order to achieve the godly life that God desires. Look what God is trying to give you by knowing the truth of His will. Is there anything here you don't want? Remember, you're the beneficiary of Jesus' will and he wants you to have the best.

2 Peter 1:3-9

'His divine power has given us <u>everything we need for a godly life through our knowledge of Him</u> who called us by his own glory and goodness. Through these he has given us his very great and

precious promises, so that through them you may participate in the divine nature, having escaped the corruption in the world caused by evil desires. For this very reason, <u>make every effort to add to your faith</u> goodness; and to goodness, knowledge; and to godliness, mutual affection; and to mutual affection, love. For if you possess these qualities in increasing measure; they will keep you from being ineffective and unproductive in your knowledge of our Lord Jesus Christ. But whoever does not have them is nearsighted and blind, forgetting that they have been cleansed from their past sins. '

I want to remind you that Jesus' apostles received His last will and wrote it down by inspiration of the Holy Spirit. The written word is referred to as scripture, or that which has been scripted or written down. Scripture has been inspired by God who used the mind, thoughts and words of the writer to guild him to write down exactly what God wanted to convey to the reader. As I previously mentioned, many of these prophets wrote down things they did not understand. Some of the promises and events about which they wrote were fulfilled hundreds of years in the future.

Here's an example of how specific God can be. Jerusalem had been destroyed and the Jews taken into Babylonian captivity by Nebuchadnezzar in 606 BC. Jeremiah was a prophet who was left in Jerusalem and wrote about a Persian King named Cyrus. He wrote that Cyrus would return the Jews to Jerusalem then rebuild the temple that was destroyed by Nebuchadnezzar. Now catch this; Cyrus was named by Jeremiah over seventy years before he came to power as the Persian King. Can you predict who will be president in 70 years and write down exactly what he will do? Jeremiah did as he was carried along and inspired by the Holy Spirit.

Ezra 1:1

'In the first year of Cyrus king of Persia, in order to fulfill the word of the Lord spoken by Jeremiah, the Lord moved the heart of Cyrus king of Persia to make a proclamation throughout his realm and also to put it in writing: "This is what Cyrus king of

Persia says: "'The Lord, the God of heaven, has given me all the kingdoms of the earth and he has appointed me to build a temple for Him at Jerusalem in Judah. '

2 Timothy 3:16-17

'All Scripture is God-breathed and is useful for teaching, rebuking, correcting and training in righteousness, so that the servant of God may be thoroughly equipped for every good work.'

We see that scripture is God-breathed (inspired) and is useful for teaching, rebuking, correcting and training so that you can be thoroughly equipped for every good work and for knowing how to receive salvation. So let me ask you, if the Bible equips you for every good work, do you need additional revelations and visions to make you complete spiritually? No! Do you need the Book of Mormon written in 1830 to make you complete spiritually? No! Do you need church traditions, manuals, creed books or confessions of faith to make you complete spiritually? No!

The scripture is all we need to make us complete spiritually. We simply have to read it because we can understand it and then we need to humbly accept it and do what it instructs us to do. No other source is needed as your religious authority. No man, creed, or council can supersede or change the scripture. It's the "legal document" and the last will and we are the beneficiaries. Embrace it. Don't get angry because it challenges your beliefs or conduct. Put it into practice and obey it.

Hebrews 5:9

He became the source of eternal salvation for all who obey Him.

IV. Conclusion

I hope you understand by now that the New Testament is God's message for us today. The Law of Moses was given to Israel and its purpose was to lead us to Christ. Now that Christ has come, we are no longer under that harsh school master. The Law of Moses could not set us free from sin and death, but Jesus can.

The Old Testament still should be studied because you really can't get the whole picture of what God did in history unless you do. It's full of important messages and shows how God honored faith and godly living and how seriously he takes disloyalty to Him. He's a jealous God and wants our love for Him to be as committed as His is for us.

God gave His word to Jesus and as His last will and testament; He made the apostles the executors who wrote it down exactly as He wanted and guided them by the Holy Spirit. When we read it, we can understand it and need to humbly accept and do it! Ready for more? Great!

Chapter 5 – Answering the Gospel Call

"Come to Me, all you who labor and are heavy laden, and I will give you rest. Take My yoke upon you and learn from Me, for I am gentle and lowly in heart, and you will find rest for your souls. For My yoke is easy and My burden is light" (Matthew11:28-30).

You should know by now that God loves you passionately and wants a relationship with you for eternity. In order to be in that relationship, you need to be a follower of Jesus, which He calls a disciple. Many think that Jesus had only twelve disciples which were the Apostles. But the followers of Jesus in the Bible were referred to as *disciples.* Followers of Jesus were called Christians only three times in the New Testament which began as a derogatory term, but the term disciple is used over 270 times. But have you ever wondered what a disciple really is? Jesus calls men and women to be His disciples, yet many times we have not really considered what He is asking or what He requires in order to answer His invitation. In this chapter, we will examine what being a disciple of Jesus is all about and show from the Bible what Jesus expects of those who desire to follow Him. Remember, the gift is free, but it's conditional.

But before we begin, let's review your relationship with Christ so you will have a clear idea of where you are and what, if anything, you might do to improve this relationship. I'm going to ask you to grab a pen and jot down some information. Take this part really serious and do it!

- Do you believe that Jesus is the Divine Son of God and that God raised Him from the dead?_____
- Are you now, or have you ever been saved? _____

Now think about this seriously. If you answered 'no' then let's see how to resolve that pretty quickly. But, if you answered 'yes' you need to examine this because as we mentioned above a lot of people might be telling you things in the Last Will of Jesus that aren't there.

If you answered yes, how were you saved (time, age, event, location, circumstances etc). Use the life-line below. Let's say you were "saved" at age 25 when you made an 'altar call' and invited Jesus into your life. Put the 'x' on the line at that point. Perhaps you were 'christened' as a baby. Put that 'x' on the line. May-be you're not sure. That's OK, because that is the reason for this chapter. Have you been baptized? Put that 'x' on the line and how you were baptized and why. Was it a year after your altar call, or when you were christened as a baby before you believed? There are different things being taught and I want you to see what's actually in the New Covenant of Jesus. I can't stress the importance of doing this simple exercise. You'll gain great value as we go through this together. Here are different scenarios that people are taught. I left one blank for you to fill in. We'll review yours later in our time together. Just be honest with yourself. Get your pen and write your own story. Just you and God can see!

Your Life Line?___x_____x_____
      Baptised as infant (Saved)   Believe/confirmed

Your Life Line?_____x_____x_____
      Believe, invite Jesus in/ sinner's prayer   Baptised as outward sign

Your Life Line?_____

The Gospel of Christ
The Gospel, God's good news to us, is the written message He uses to save us. It's the story of the death, burial and resurrection of Christ and our response to that message. Remember, we're the beneficiaries of His will and the reward for us is eternal life. The Gospel message is the power which God uses to give us the information to understand His will and ultimately save us. Think about it. If you are the recipient of a Ten Million dollar estate, but no one tells you about it or how to claim it, you never receive the benefits of what you're entitled to. Plus if the will stipulates that you must come to Denver, Colorado and present two

forms of identification and be a legal citizen, the benefit is still free, but there are conditions that you must meet. You understand that, right? Conditions required to receive a free gift don't mean you earn it! Well, the gift of Christ is also free, but there are conditions you must meet.

> Romans 1:16

> 'For I am not ashamed of the gospel, because it is the power of God that brings salvation to everyone who believes: first to the Jew, then to the Gentile. '

> John 20:30-31

> 'Jesus performed many other signs in the presence of his disciples, which are not recorded in this book. But <u>these are written that you may believe that Jesus is the Messiah, the Son of God, and that by believing you may have life in his name</u>.'

I want to stress again to you that the written will is what gives you the information and truth that offers you, as the beneficiary, eternal life. Jesus did a lot more than what was recorded, but be assured that you have more than enough information and truth to spend eternity with God. And as you already read in the previous chapter, putting His message into obedient action is one of the conditions for you as a beneficiary. No action; no salvation! You must respond.

The Lordship of Jesus

When you call Jesus your 'Lord' it means you acknowledge Him as your Master, and understand that you are His servant; His free slave; His disciple. You're basically surrendering control of your life to Him.

A term used by Paul to describe our relationship with Jesus as Lord is *bond servant*. "Paul, a bond servant of Christ Jesus, called as an apostle, set apart for the gospel of God" (Romans 1:1). So let's explore this relationship between Jesus as Lord and Master and you as free slaves or bond servant.

In Old Testament times let's assume you are financially destitute and unable to support yourself. There is no social assistance, but there is a way for you to be able to feed and clothe yourself. You can volunteer to become someone's servant or slave. This isn't the same idea as involuntary slavery that happened in our history. You could volunteer to become someone's slave/servant, but at the end of seven years, that relationship ended and you were again free.

Now, after seven years, let's assume that you still had no means to support yourself. Your master is obligated to set you free, but if you love your master then you would have the option of becoming his slave voluntarily and permanently. The procedure for doing so is that the master would bring you to a door or doorpost and you would have your ear pierced with an awl. This ceremony symbolized the voluntary life-long relationship you entered into with your master whom you love and wanted to serve for the rest of your life.

> Exodus 21:5-6
>
> *But if the slave plainly says, 'I love my master, my wife and my children; I will not go out as a free man,' then his master shall bring him to God (or the judges who acted in God's name) then he shall bring him to the door or the doorpost. And his master shall pierce his ear with an awl; and he shall serve him permanently.*

This portrays the voluntary relationship we enter into when we acknowledge Jesus as our Lord and we become His bond servants permanently. He paid an extremely high price to purchase you as His own possession – death on a cross and as you willingly submit to His Lordship in your life you must remember the value He places on you. He's not a tyrant slave owner, but a loving master, but He's still the Lord and you're the slave in this relationship.

> Matthew 11:28-30
>
> *'"Come to Me, all who are weary and heavy-laden, and I will give you rest. Take My yoke upon you and learn from Me, for I am gentle and humble in heart, and you will find rest for your souls. For My yoke is easy and My burden is light." '*

Once you enter into this discipleship relationship with Jesus, your priorities change totally. It's no longer about you, it's all about Him.

You no longer live your life for yourself, but you live your life for your new Master – Jesus. Think of it this way. You now live your life the way Jesus would live your life. You are the kind of husband Jesus would be to your wife. You are the kind of employee or boss Jesus would be in your position. You pay your taxes honestly the way Jesus would pay your taxes. You imitate Him in your life. You now live your life for Him.

2 Corinthians 5:15

And He died for all, so that they who live might no longer live for themselves, but for Him who died and rose again on their behalf.

Philippians 1:21

For me to live is Christ.

When you truly understand the intimacy of this new relationship, you understand that you and Christ are now one. He is in you and you are in Him. The relationship is unlike anything any two humans can have.

John 15:5-8

I am the vine, you are the branches; he who abides in Me and I in him, he bears much fruit, for apart from Me you can do nothing. My Father is glorified by this, that you bear much fruit, and so prove to be My disciples. If you abide in Me, and My words abide in you, ask whatever you wish, and it will be done for you.

As you're about to learn, a disciple is not just a term or title, but a mind-set and commitment. A disciple studies his Master. He not only studies his masters' lessons, but his master *IS the lesson.* His goal is to become like his master, and to imitate his master. When you look at a true disciple, you can see who his master is because he becomes just like his master. At that point, he is the student, and a disciple.

Jesus commissioned the apostles, "Go into all the world and make disciples of all nations..." (Matthew 28:18). In order to be a disciple, obedience to the Master is paramount. The disciple – Lord Relationship is what makes it happen.

Luke 6:46

"Why do you call me, 'Lord, Lord,' and do not do what I say? As for everyone who comes to me and hears my words and puts them into practice, I will show you what they are like. They are like a man building a house, who dug down deep and laid the foundation on rock. When a flood came, the torrent struck that house but could not shake it, because it was well built. But the one who hears my words and does not put them into practice is like a man who built a house on the ground without a foundation. The moment the torrent struck that house, it collapsed and its destruction was complete."'

When you call Jesus 'Lord' you are submitting yourself to a Lord – servant relationship. He is your Master and you are His obedient servant. This is one of the conditions of the will but remember it's nothing you earn. The gift is free and at His invitation, but it is conditional and the decision to accept those conditions is left totally up to you. Follow or not follow. God's a gentleman and won't force you.

Lip-service in this relationship won't cut it. Jesus knows if you're genuine. You can argue, justify, maneuver, but if you don't submit to Jesus as your legitimate Lord to do the father's will, He knows you're a fake.

Matthew 7:21-23

"Not everyone who says to me, 'Lord, Lord,' will enter the kingdom of heaven, but <u>only the one who does the will of my Father who is in heaven</u>. Many will say to me on that day, 'Lord, Lord, did we not prophesy in your name and in your name drive out demons and in your name perform many miracles?' Then I will tell them plainly, 'I never knew you. Away from me, you evildoers!"

I think this is one of the most sobering verses in the Bible for me as a disciple of Jesus. Am I doing the will of his Father or just calling Him 'Lord, Lord?' I prophesied or taught in your name Lord. I drove out demons and performed miracles. But we aren't saved by religious things we do, we're saved by our relationship to Him as Lord/Servant. Doing miracles and driving out demons are cool things, right? But they are no verification that He knows you in the sense of a relationship.

Hebrews 5:8-9

'He became the source of eternal salvation for all who obey Him.'

Obedience to Him as your Lord is part of the requirements of being a disciple. Don't misunderstand this and think that you have to be perfect or sinless because you never will be in this life. Obedience is an act of submission to your Master and the understanding that He owns you as His servant; and you're owned by a very loving Master who has your best interest and eternal life as His only priority in your life.

What is faith?

Many falsely think that if they only *believe* things about Jesus they can be saved. I call this the "Santa Syndrome." If I believe in Santa there will be a gift under the tree for me. After all, doesn't John 3:16 say, "For God so loved the world that whoever believes in Him shall not perish but have eternal life?" Yes, it does, but the idea of belief carries with it a deeper meaning than simple mental acknowledgement of who He is. Don't be deceived into thinking if you simply believe in Santa Jesus there will be a gift of eternal life waiting under the tree of life when you die. After all, the devil and all his demons believe who Jesus is. Remember the demon possessed man in the synagogue? Here is the demons' response to Jesus, '"What do you want with us, Jesus of Nazareth? Have you come to destroy us? I know who you are—the Holy One of God!" (Mark 1:24).

James 2:19

You believe that there is one God. Good! Even the demons believe that—and shudder.

Jesus warns us that the way to eternal life is very narrow and only a few will find it. I suspect that our politically correct socialistic preconception of God causes us to believe that He's so loving that He could not and would not exclude anyone from heaven. "Uncle Bob was a good guy and is now he's in better place playing cards with his ol buddies next to the pearly gates!" Everybody is a great person when they die and at the funeral eulogy, everybody is in heaven.

Remember, that this loving God killed the entire world in a flood. This loving God killed the first born children in the entire nation of Egypt. This loving God promises that anyone whose name is not in the Lamb's book of life will be cast into the lake of fire along with the devil and his angels. Pay attention here! He who has ears; are you listening?

> *Matthew 7:13-14*
>
> *'"Enter through the narrow gate; for the gate is wide and the way is broad that leads to destruction, and there are many who enter through it. For the gate is small and the way is narrow that leads to life, and there are few who find it. '*

Belief is not the same as faith. Jesus brought in a system of grace-truth; or the truth about grace. This new covenant of grace-truth offers eternal salvation and forgiveness, but faith, trust and obedience are components of this system of grace. You can't earn it by being good enough or "paying off your sins" or by saying prayers or burning candles or doing community service as an act of "penance." Grace is Gods' offer, but faith is your acceptance of that offer.

> *Ephesians 2:8-9*
>
> *'For it is by grace you have been saved, through faith—and this is not from yourselves, it is the gift of God— not by works, so that no one can boast. '*
>
> *Hebrews 11:6*
>
> *'And <u>without faith it is impossible to please God</u>, because anyone who comes to Him must believe that he exists and that he rewards those who earnestly seek Him. '*

Let's examine the part that works or action has in legitimate Biblical faith.

James 2:14-17; 24-26

'What good is it, my brothers and sisters, if someone claims to have faith but has no deeds? Can such faith save them? In the same way, <u>faith by itself, if it is not accompanied by action, is dead.</u> But someone will say, "You have faith; I have deeds." Show me your faith without deeds, and I will show you my faith by my deeds.

You see that a person is considered righteous by what they do and <u>not by faith alone. As the body without the spirit is dead, so faith without deeds is dead.</u>'

This concept has caused some confusion throughout Christianity and you may be wincing right now as they read this! That reaction is in response to the "works and penance" mentality promoted by some that teach that you have to "work off your sin through penance."

We are saved by grace through faith and not by works, but faith without works is dead and will not save us. So please pay attention here. This is really important! Merit or doing good works to offset our sins doesn't add brownie points to the Book of Life on our behalf, but faith without putting it into practice is of no value. This isn't a contradiction but needs some clarification if you haven't explored this before. Let's examine this deeper and try to make sense of it. Are your ears hearing? Good, let's continue.

Hebrews chapter eleven is called "Faith's Hall of Fame" because it lists several examples of people who demonstrated what faith really was. None of the people in this chapter were super religious and definitely not sinless, yet they were commended by God for their faith and used as examples of what faith looks like. Abraham was a liar; Moses was a murderer; Rahab was a hooker and Noah was a drunk. They, like us, were all sinners, yet they were justified by their faith because of the actions they took when God told them to do something.

Hebrews 11:7

'By faith Noah, when warned about things not yet seen, in holy fear built an ark to save his family. By his faith he condemned the world and became heir of the righteousness that is in keeping with faith.

God was disgusted with the human race for how corrupt they had become. However, He chose Noah to save a remnant of humanity and did a "reboot" of sorts. Look carefully at what Noah did. God told Him to build an ark, though Noah had never seen rain; never seen a flood and may have frowned a bit wondering why God was asking him to do this. He didn't ask God for the details of how he was supposed to gather all the animals, and it took Him a hundred years to complete this project. One hundred years of labor to build an aircraft carrier for animals. That's a lot of work, don't you agree? Noah was doing all this by blind faith. He never before saw the things that God warned him were coming, but he trusted and he just did it!

Notice the sequence of how faith works. God commanded; Noah obeyed and put into action what was commanded even though he didn't understand it all and it resulted in the salvation of his family. Noah was probably ridiculed by his neighbors and extended family, but he just did it because God said to do it.

Noah could have tried to say a "Sinkers prayer" instead of obeying what God told Him to do. But, God didn't tell Him to say a prayer, he told Him to build a boat. Noah could have reasoned, "God I'll be a really good person to pay off the evil I've done," and attempted to earn God's favor. However, you can never be good enough to earn your salvation. God told Noah to build a boat and it took a hundred years of blood, sweat and tears, but it was in no way meritorious. Here's the faith formula:

God's command
+ trusting obedience put into action
= Faith that saves.

Let's look at another example – Moses and the Passover. Israel had been in Egypt four hundred and thirty years by this time and they were now under great oppression by Pharaoh. God sent Moses to Pharaoh on nine occasions with the message, "Let my people go!" Pharaoh stubbornly refused those nine attempts.

The tenth attempt was a horrible plague God used to finally break Pharaohs' resolve. He would send a destroyer through the land and kill the firstborn of every family, including all the livestock. Moses was given a command by God to protect the people of Israel and it was a pretty strange command. Every Jewish household was to prepare a meal and get ready to leave immediately. They were to kill a young lamb and take its' blood and smear it over the door header and down the side posts. "OK kids, let's help daddy spread little Billy's' blood on our door and wash your hands for dinner, cause we're going on a big trip tomorrow!" The destroyer would "Passover" the houses covered in the blood of the lamb but deal harsh judgment to every house without the blood. Their firstborn were about to die that night.

When the destroyer visited during the night, every Egyptian household including Pharaohs' received the judgment of God while every Jewish household covered by the blood was saved.

Did you see the faith formula again?

> **God's command**
> **+ trusting obedience put into action**
> **= Faith that saves.**

Let's look at one more, the destruction of Jericho. This is a very strange battle plan, but God wanted to show that the battle belongs to the Lord, not to our human effort. God promised to give the land to Abraham over four hundred years earlier. In order to possess the land, the fortified cities would have to be captured or destroyed. The first city, Jericho, was a heavily fortified city with massive walls to protect it. Joshua, Moses' successor, calls the people together and gives this speech. "So here's the battle plan Generals. I want the people to march around the city walls silently once a day for six days. On the seventh day, march around the city silently six times, then stop on the seventh, shout and blow the trumpets!" Can you see the priests and the leaders looking at each other with Joshua's brilliant battle plan? "Anything else sir?" "Nope, God said this will guarantee that the city will be ours. Carry on!" Again, pretty unusual command, don't you agree? But the walls fell from the inside out when they did what God said to do. "God chooses the foolish things of this world to confound the wise!"

Hebrews 11:30

*'By faith the walls of Jericho fell, **after** the army had marched around them for seven days. '*

Did you see the faith formula again?

God's command
+ trusting obedience put into action
= Faith that saves.

I hope by now you understand how we're saved by grace through faith. We are not saved by trying to do good stuff to off-set the scales. It doesn't work that way. But you also need to understand that we're not just saved by believing. We have to put into action what God commands. Had Noah not built an ark, he would have perished. He obeyed God's command without understand it all and by his obedient faith in action he was saved. The Israelites each killed a lamb and spread its blood on the doors as commanded, and they were saved by their obedient faith without understanding it all. By faith the walls of Jericho fell after they walked around them for seven days as God commanded. Faith without deeds is dead.

Those commands were given to those people at that time for a specific reason and not to us. You can smear lambs blood on your door today, but don't expect God to save you if you do. If a battle commander marches around a city and blows some trumpets, he's probably going to go down in history as a fool. We have to examine the commands that are part of the New Covenant that do apply to us today. Then we simply apply the faith formula:

God's command
+ trusting obedience put into action
= Faith that saves.

II. The Requirements of Discipleship

When Jesus gave The Great Commission to His apostles He told them this:

Matthew 28:18-10

'Then Jesus came to them and said, "All authority in heaven and on earth has been given to me. Therefore go and make disciples of all nations, baptizing them in the name of the Father and of the Son and of the Holy Spirit, and teaching them to obey everything I have commanded you. And surely I am with you always, to the very end of the age."'

The term in English "make disciples" is actually more of a verb, "go disciple the nations." Two participles in this verse tell how to *disciple* the nations – baptizing them and teaching them to obey. More on this later, but for now let's look at what Jesus required of those who wanted to become disciples of His.

Luke 14:25-35

'Large crowds were traveling with Jesus, and turning to them he said: "If anyone comes to me and does not hate father and mother, wife and children, brothers and sisters—yes, even their own life—such a person cannot be my disciple. And whoever does not carry their cross and follow me cannot be my disciple. "Suppose one of you wants to build a tower. Won't you first sit down and estimate the cost to see if you have enough money to complete it? For if you lay the foundation and are not able to finish it, everyone who sees it will ridicule you, saying, 'This person began to build and wasn't able to finish.' "Or suppose a

king is about to go to war against another king. Won't he first sit down and consider whether he is able with ten thousand men to oppose the one coming against Him with twenty thousand? If he is not able, he will send a delegation while the other is still a long way off and will ask for terms of peace. In the same way, those of you who do not give up everything you have cannot be my disciples. "Salt is good, but if it loses its saltiness, how can it be made salty again? It is fit neither for the soil nor for the manure pile; it is thrown out. "Whoever has ears to hear, let them hear."

I don't know what you're thinking as you read this section, but the first time I read it I was shocked. It seemed as though Jesus was trying to scare people away rather than draw them in. You'll rarely, if ever, hear preachers today telling people this message about the requirements of being a disciple of Jesus. Let's examine them in order.

Total allegiance to Jesus
Jesus says that if you want to follow Him, then you must *hate* your mother, father and even your own life or you cannot be his disciple. Wow; pretty strong language! He's not saying you must hate in the sense of anger or malice, but in the sense of loving them and yourself less when compared to your unquestioning allegiance to Him as your Lord. When a slave had his ear pierced and became the permanent servant of his master, his allegiance was ONLY to his master. Mom, dad, friends and spouse were all secondary from now on.

> *Matthew 10:37*
>
> *"Anyone who loves their father or mother more than me is not worthy of me; anyone who loves their son or daughter more than me is not worthy of me."*

He's requiring your total and undiluted allegiance. No one can serve two masters. Either Jesus is in first place or He will have no place in your life. You must love Him more than family, friends and even your own life. The commitment is total or nothing.

When people follow Jesus, it carries with it sometimes violent reactions from others. Around the world today, there are thousands of followers of Christ who are beaten, imprisoned and killed simply because they are believers in Him. That's why Jesus is telling you the commitment needed before you start the journey. Those you love may end up hating you because of your faith in Christ and if you don't have a solid allegiance in your heart before you start, you will fail.

> *Matthew 10:21-22*
>
> *"Brother will betray brother to death, and a father his child; children will rebel against their parents and have them put to death. You will be hated by everyone because of me, but the one who stands firm to the end will be saved. '*

Are you willing to make that commitment? If you want to be a beneficiary of eternal life then you have no choice. That's the deal and that's the condition.

Death to sin and self

Jesus then requires you to carry your own cross. What does that mean? He's not asking you to put a symbol of a cross around your neck; and isn't asking you to carry a wooden cross around. Crosses were an implement of capital punishment – an instrument of death. When you carried a cross, you were going to die. It would be like Jesus telling you that if you want to be his disciple, you had to first take a lethal injection. But He does not want you to commit suicide like some cult leader. But a death must occur. The death that Jesus requires is a death to sin and self. The apostle Paul (once Saul of Tarsus, the persecutor of followers of Jesus) said this:

> *Galatians 2:20*
>
> *'I have been crucified with Christ and **I no longer live**, but Christ lives in me. The life I now live in the body, I live by faith in the Son of God, who loved me and gave Himself for me. '*

Did you catch it? Paul now considered Himself dead – "I no longer live but Christ now lives in me." When you become a disciple of Jesus, it's no longer about you; it's all about Him. It's no longer about living for your flesh because you no longer belong to yourself, but to King Jesus.

1 Corinthians 6:19-20

'Or do you not know that your body is a temple of the Holy Spirit who is in you, whom you have from God, and that <u>you are not your own? For you have been bought with a price</u> therefore glorify God in your body. '

Romans 6:4-7; 11-14

For we know that <u>our old self was crucified</u> with Him so that the body ruled by sin might be done away with, that we should no longer be slaves to sin— because anyone who has died has been set free from sin. '

'In the same way, <u>count yourselves dead to sin but alive to God in Christ Jesus</u>. Therefore do not let sin reign in your mortal body so that you obey its evil desires. Do not offer any part of yourself to sin as an instrument of wickedness, but rather offer yourselves to God as those who have been brought from death to life; and <u>offer every part of yourself to Him as an instrument of righteousness</u>. For sin shall no longer be your master, because you are not under the law, but under grace. '

Romans 8:13

'For if you live according to the flesh, you will die; but if by the Spirit you put to death the misdeeds of the body, you will live. '

When you take up your cross to follow Jesus, sin is no longer your master because you are under grace. You also are no longer the master of your universe – Jesus is. It's a matter of control. So let me ask you, are you willing to let your life be totally controlled by Jesus? Whoever does not take up his cross daily and follow cannot be a disciple.

The consideration is serious

In the above passage (Luke 14:28-32) Jesus gives two illustrations to help us count the cost and think seriously about the decision to follow Him. The first is that of a man building a tower who needed to count the cost to make sure he had enough material to finish the project. If he didn't, it would mock Him.

I remember driving near Canyon Ferry Lake by Helena, Montana and viewing a house someone had started years before, but it was never finished. It was framed, but never sided or completed. Year after year I watched this house deteriorate and thought about this verse. Here was a man who started a building, but for one reason or another he never finished it. I guess you could say, "Look before you leap," when it comes to starting your journey with Jesus. Finish what you start.

The second illustration is that of a military leader preparing to go to war with ten thousand soldiers and his opponent has twenty thousand. Two to One odds aren't a good bet when going to war. Realizing it's a bad battle strategy; he sends a delegation and asks for terms of peace while his enemy is still a long way off. Once you start your relationship with Jesus, finish it! Look before you leap, but neutrality and indecision is not an option. You will either do battle with God on the judgment day, at which time you will lose for eternity, or accept terms of peace. The choice is yours, but the consequences of your choice are not yours.

The cost is everything

Then Jesus concludes with this, "In the same way <u>anyone who does not give up everything he has cannot be my disciple.</u>" Is Jesus here asking us to be homeless and poor? Consider this question, "What do slaves own?" Nothing; right? They don't even own themselves. The idea is that when you surrender to Jesus as your loving Master, you become His servant and you surrender your life and everything you own and He now owns it all. You no longer live, but Christ lives in you and the life you then live, you live by faith in the one who died and gave Himself up for you to give you eternal life. That's the best investment you'll ever make in eternity, but it does require total unconditional surrender.

You're invited, but will you accept?

> Luke 14:16-24
>
> 'But He said to him, "A man was giving a big dinner, and he invited many; and at the dinner hour he sent his slave to say to those who had been invited, 'Come; for everything is ready now.' <u>But they all alike began to make excuses</u>. The first one said to

him, 'I have bought a piece of land and I need to go out and look at it; please consider me excused.' Another one said, 'I have bought five yoke of oxen, and I am going to try them out; please consider me excused.' Another one said, 'I have married a wife, and for that reason I cannot come.' And the slave came back and reported this to his master. Then the head of the household became angry and said to his slave, 'Go out at once into the streets and lanes of the city and bring in here the poor and crippled and blind and lame.' And the slave said, 'Master, what you commanded has been done, and still there is room.' And the master said to the slave, 'Go out into the highways and along the hedges, and compel them to come in, so that my house may be filled. For I tell you, none of those men who were invited shall taste of my dinner.'" '

The invitation Jesus is offering you is to sit with Him at the Great Banquet in heaven and enjoy eternal life. There's room for all and He's got an invitation with your name on it, but will you accept? One man was concerned with his investments. The other was more concerned with his business and the third was more concerned with his relationships and family. What's your excuse? I'll guarantee you that one billion years from now if you ignore His invitation, you'll wish you had accepted. Eternity is a long time.

In order to be a disciple of Jesus, He wants you to carefully consider the conditions. It's totally free, and at the same time costs a great deal that you must first consider. Your allegiance to Him is first above friends, family, sin, self and possessions. When you give it all, you then gain everything including eternal life.

Before his encounter on the road to Damascus, Paul was a prominent religious leader and fairly well off financially and socially. But, when he started his relationship with Christ as his Lord, things changed. He considered everything a total loss in order to gain Christ.

Philippians 3:7-11

'But whatever were gains to me I now consider loss for the sake of Christ. What is more, I consider everything a loss because of the surpassing worth of knowing Christ Jesus my Lord, for whose sake I have lost all things. I consider them garbage, that I may gain Christ and be found in Him, not having a righteousness of my own that comes from the law, but that which is through faith in Christ—the righteousness that comes from God on the basis of faith. I want to know Christ—yes, to know the power of his resurrection and participation in his sufferings, becoming like Him in his death, and so, somehow, attaining to the resurrection from the dead. '

III. Being United with Christ

Now we're going to examine what the New Covenant tells us we must do in order to be united with Christ. How does the relationship start? What I'm about to show you from the Bible is rarely taught in churches or on TV. Just like the requirements Jesus laid out on discipleship, so the process of getting "into Christ" is not shared and is mostly ignored. This is where referring back to your life line will come in. Let's begin.

When Jesus commissioned His apostles to go into all the world and disciple the nations He told them the process was to baptize them and teach them to obey everything He had commanded (Matthew 20:18-20). Now let's see the verses where that is taught under the New Covenant.

The New Covenant went into force the moment Jesus died. He was with the Apostles for forty days, and then ascended back to heaven to take His seat at the Right Hand of God on the throne of David from which He now reigns as King of Kings and Lord of Lords. The day of Pentecost finally arrives; the apostles are baptized with the Holy Spirit and begin teaching the Gospel for the very first time in languages they had never before learned. We have the written record of Peter's speech, but understand that the other eleven are also teaching different groups throughout the crowd that gathered for the day of Pentecost.

Peter shows from Old Testament prophecies, that Jesus is the one spoken of through the prophet David that he was not abandoned to the grave, neither did his flesh see decay and that God had in fact made this Jesus whom you (the Jews) crucified both Lord and Christ. His sermon hit dead center and notice their question and Peter's response:

Acts 2:36-42

*'Therefore let all the house of Israel know for certain that God has made Him both Lord and Christ-this Jesus whom you crucified." Now when they heard this, they were pierced to the heart, and said to Peter and the rest of the apostles, "**Brethren, what shall we do?**" Peter said to them, "Repent, and each of you be baptized in the name of Jesus Christ for the forgiveness of your sins; and you will receive the gift of the Holy Spirit. For the promise is for you and your children and for all who are far off, as many as the Lord our God will call to Himself." And with many other words he solemnly testified and kept on exhorting them, saying, "Be saved from this perverse generation!" So then, those who had received his word were baptized; and that day there were added about three thousand souls. '*

What Peter preached is exactly what Jesus commanded them to preach. Now, if you watch any TV preacher speak to a crowd of people, what do you hear them say? "Let me lead you in the sinner's prayer and invite

Jesus into your heart." Peter didn't preach that, and Jesus never told anyone to preach that. You make disciples by first baptizing them.

What did the people receive when they were baptized? It says "for the forgiveness of your sins; and you will receive the gift of the Holy Spirit." Remember its sin that causes us to be lost in the first place. "All have sinned and fallen short of the glory of God, and the wages of sin is death" (Romans 3:23; 6:23). So, until a person's sins are forgiven, they remain under the death penalty. Peter said that when the people repented (changed their minds and turned to

God) and were baptized their sins would be forgiven and they would receive the Holy Spirit.

Keep reading to verses 40-41. Peter kept exhorting them to be saved! *"Then those who received his message were baptized, about three thousand of them."* It's the same faith formula we've seen.

God's command
+ trusting obedience put into action
= Faith that saves.

Let's examine some more scripture.

Romans 6:3-7

*'Or do you not know that all of us who have been <u>baptized **into Christ**</u> Jesus have been baptized into His death? Therefore we have been buried with Him through baptism into death, so that as Christ was raised from the dead through the glory of the Father, so we too might walk in newness of life. For if we have become **<u>united</u>** with Him in the likeness of His death, certainly we shall also be in the likeness of His resurrection, knowing this, that our old self was crucified with Him, in order that our body of sin might be done away with, so that we would no longer be slaves to sin; for he who has died is freed from sin. '*

Paul says that we are baptized "into Christ." In this act of obedient faith, God unites us with Christ. Our old man dies with Christ, is buried with Christ, and is raised with Christ to walk in a new life.

Under the Abrahamic covenant, circumcision was given as a seal of the covenant relationship with God. In the following verses, Paul says that we also were circumcised, but not a physical circumcision done by human hands. Our flesh (referring to our sin) is miraculously removed by God when we are buried with Him in baptism and raised up with Him **through faith in the working of God who raised Him from the dead.**

Colossians 2:12

"In Him you were also circumcised with <u>a circumcision</u> <u>made</u> <u>without hands, in the removal of the body of the flesh by the</u> <u>circumcision of Christ; having been buried with Him in baptism,</u> in which you were also raised up with Him <u>through faith in the</u> <u>working of God,</u> who raised Him from the dead. '

Earlier, we talked about the Covenant made with Abraham in Genesis chapter twelve. The promise was that through one of his descendants all the nations of the earth would be blessed. In order to be a recipient of this blessing, you had to also be a seed of Abraham. Look how baptism makes all this happen.

Galatians 3:26-27

'For you are all sons of God through faith in Christ Jesus. <u>For all</u> <u>of you who were baptized into Christ have clothed yourselves</u> <u>with Christ.</u> There is neither Jew nor Greek, there is neither slave nor free man, there is neither male nor female; for you are all one in Christ Jesus. <u>And if you belong to Christ, then you are</u> <u>Abraham's descendants, heirs according to promise. '</u>

So from what we've learned so far, when do we receive forgiveness of sins and the gift of the indwelling of the Holy Spirit - When we're baptized. When are we united with and placed "into" Christ - When we're baptized. When does God perform a miraculous surgery to circumcise and remove the flesh - When we're baptized. When do we by faith become sons of God, clothe ourselves in Christ and become Abraham's descendants and thus heirs according to promise - When we're baptized.

Now, some may say, "Baptism doesn't save you, Jesus does!" Let me ask you this question "Did the ark save Noah or did God?" Did the blood of the lamb on the door post save the Israelites, or did God? Remember the faith formula. God saves us when we put obedient faith in action.

God's command
+ trusting obedience put into action
= Faith that saves.

1 Peter 3:20-21

..the patience of God kept waiting in the days of Noah, during the construction of the ark, in which a few, that is, eight persons, were brought safely through the water. Corresponding to that, <u>baptism now saves you</u>-not the removal of dirt from the flesh, but an appeal to God for a good conscience-through the resurrection of Jesus Christ"

So, just like the ark saved Noah, baptism saves you. Why? Because that's the way God chooses to do it. Baptism is more than simply getting wet and removing dirt from your flesh. In fact you might get baptized in a muddy river and come up filthy. It's not washing the flesh, it's the appeal to God for a clean conscience and it's tied to the resurrection of Jesus. Under the New Covenant, God chooses water baptism as the obedient faith action before He will forgive sins and seal a person with the Holy Spirit. Those are the terms in the will.

Mark 16:15-16

'And He said to them, "Go into all the world and preach the gospel to all creation. He who has believed and has been baptized shall be saved..."

If you recall the conversion story of Saul of Tarsus, he was a zealous Pharisee with authority to persecute Christians. While he was headed to Damascus Jesus appeared to Him after the resurrection and the Bible records he became blind with scales on his eyes. He was led by the hand of his colleagues into the city and didn't sleep eat or drink anything for three days. What do you think he was doing for those three days? I can bet he was weeping in anguish and crying out to God for forgiveness, don't you agree?

So here's a man, deeply convicted praying and fasting three days and nights for God's mercy. Surely by asking God for forgiveness and mourning that must have given Him forgiveness, right? Well, three days later a man named Ananias came to Him and told Him the conditions of forgiveness commissioned by Jesus.

Acts 22:12-16

"'A certain Ananias, a man who was devout by the standard of the Law, and well spoken of by all the Jews who lived there, came to me, and standing near said to me, 'Brother Saul, receive your sight!' And at that very time I looked up at Him. And he said, 'The God of our fathers has appointed you to know His will and to see the Righteous One and to hear an utterance from His mouth. For you will be a witness for Him to all men of what you have seen and heard. <u>Now why do you delay? Get up and be baptized, and wash away your sins, calling on His name.'</u>

Obeying God in baptism is "calling on the name of the Lord." Paul had seen the risen Christ and fasted for three days and nights and yet his sins were not forgiven until he had them washed away by this obedient work of faith (Colossians 2:11-12). A person is not saved until forgiveness is received; therefore a person is saved when their sins are washed away in baptism. Ananias didn't lead Him in some "sinners' prayer." He preached the Gospel that Jesus commissioned. "Whoever believes and is baptized will be saved."

What is required before being baptized?
In this discussion you will again be challenged to examine existing beliefs in different religious circles. Is sprinkling an OK substitution? What about infant baptism? Remember, be quick to listen and slow to anger. This may not be what you were taught. Accept the word humbly. Ready?

Jesus clearly stated that before salvation can be obtained that belief in Him and His Resurrection is a prerequisite. Can an infant believe those things or a better question might be "Is an infant guilty of sin?" Does a baby need to be forgiven and what did he or she do wrong by being born?

The doctrine of "original sin" teaches that we are all born totally depraved and that sin has been passed on to us by our parents. This doctrine has some serious and often not discussed consequences. Let's examine it in light of scripture.

> Psalm 51:5
>
> *'Behold, I was brought forth in iniquity, and in sin my mother conceived me.'*

This verse is often used to show that David was "born in sin." But such is not the case. The better sense of this verse is that it was David's mother who sinned when she conceived him. But let's look at some other verses that better explain. An honest question to ask is, "Am I responsible and guilty for Adam's sin and therefore is sin inherited? The answer is no!

> Ezekiel 18:20
>
> *'The person who sins will die. The son will not bear the punishment for the father's iniquity, nor will the father bear the punishment for the son's iniquity; the righteousness of the righteous will be upon himself and the wickedness of the wicked will be upon himself. '*

From this verse we learn that the person who sins is responsible for his own iniquity and not that of his father. The wickedness of a person's own decisions is credited to he himself and not to someone else. That makes perfect sense, doesn't it? So if I'm not responsible for my father's sin, how can I be responsible for Adams'? Well, I'm not and neither are you.

Now, consider this. The Bible clearly states that the wages of sin is death. So, if an infant is born guilty of sin, then dies two days later, then a just God has no option other than to condemn that child to hell forever. The Catholic Church saw this dilemma and made up another alternative – "Limbo." There is no such teaching in the Bible. The only two alternatives discussed in scripture are saved or lost; Heaven or Hell. But what has the infant done wrong? Nothing. The child didn't lie, cheat, take God's name in vain, or commit adultery. To think an infant is guilty and condemned for simply being born is absurd to any reasoning mind. In fact, Jesus used little children as examples of those who are greatest in the kingdom of heaven because of their innocent, sinless character.

Matthew 18:1-6

'At that time the disciples came to Jesus and said, "Who then is greatest in the kingdom of heaven?" And He called a child to Himself and set Him before them, and said, "Truly I say to you, unless you are converted and become like children, you will not enter the kingdom of heaven. Whoever then humbles Himself as this child, he is the greatest in the kingdom of heaven. And whoever receives one such child in My name receives Me; but whoever causes one of these little ones who believe in Me to stumble, it would be better for Him to have a heavy millstone hung around his neck, and to be drowned in the depth of the sea.

I think that pretty much settles this discussion in my mind. When asked who is the greatest in the kingdom of heaven, Jesus could find none greater than little children. Why? Because they're sinless and perfect.

Matthew 19:13-14

'Then some children were brought to Him so that He might lay His hands on them and pray; and the disciples rebuked them. But Jesus said, "Let the children alone, and do not hinder them from coming to Me for the kingdom of heaven belongs to such as these."

Here is another occurrence where Jesus chastised the disciples for trying to keep little children from coming to Jesus so he could lay hands on them and pray. Again He reassures us that the kingdom of heaven already belongs to such as these. They aren't totally depraved sinners, but rather pure, innocent and sinless.

If an infant was born in sin, then he would be required to meet the terms of pardon mandated in the New Covenant. He would be required to believe in Jesus and His resurrection, but infants can't believe. He would be required to repent and turn away from sin, but an infant can't repent. He would be required to confess with his mouth the Lordship of Jesus, but an infant can't talk. These are absurd implications. Are you with me in this? I think you see the point.

So if infants aren't born with original sin, when exactly does a person become a sinner? I don't think that question can accurately be answered, but Paul reveals when he understood that he became a sinner.

> *Romans 7:7-11*
>
> *"...I would not have come to know sin except through the Law; for I would not have known about coveting if the Law had not said, "you shall not covet." But sin, taking opportunity through the commandment, produced in me coveting of every kind; for apart from the Law sin is dead. I was once alive apart from the Law; but when the commandment came, sin became alive and I died; and this commandment, which was to result in life, proved to result in death for me; for sin, taking an opportunity through the commandment, deceived me and through it killed me."*

Paul reveals for us some important information about personal accountability and when he knew sin and it ultimately killed Him. He said he would not have come to know sin unless he knew what it was. He didn't know what coveting was until he was old enough to understand the law that taught him what it was. Before his "age of accountability" (whatever that age is) he says he was alive, and sinless. But there was a time in his life when his understanding of the law sprang into his conscious mind then sin became alive to him and he died. Sin took the opportunity through knowledge of the law, perhaps his understanding of right and wrong, and at that time the very law that was good, holy and pure killed him. He became a sinner and the wages of that sin was death. He was now in need of a Savior. But how old was he? Who knows. Obviously he wasn't 8 days old or an infant. Was he five years old? I don't think so. Perhaps twelve or thirteen? May-be. Whatever age that is for the individual, there is a time when a person becomes aware of their own sinfulness and they can't deny the knowledge of right and wrong and for some reason they choose to do the wrong thing because they know they're not supposed to. It's the "Wet paint don't touch" thing. And all of us want to touch the wet paint, and we ultimately do.

Paul was born as a Jew under the Law of Moses. However his innocent mind knew nothing of sin until that law sprang to life in his mind and he understood that he had violated God's standard of right and wrong. Before he knew right from wrong, he was alive and sinless. He wasn't aware of, "Thou Shalt Not Murder" when he was an infant, was he? He couldn't be held accountable for, "Honor thy father and mother" when he was 6 months old, could he? There had to be a time when he comprehended what he was doing and fully understood he had violated his values morals or judgment. Once he comprehended that, those values turned on him, stuck the knife of judgment in his heart and killed him and at that point he became a sinner in need of forgiveness.

Some people are raised in countries where they have no access to the Bible, so how can they sin if they don't know God's written standard for right and wrong. Glad you asked.

> *Romans 2:12-16*
>
> *'For all who have sinned without the Law will also perish without the Law, and all who have sinned under the Law will be judged by the Law; For when Gentiles who do not have the Law do instinctively the things of the Law, these, not having the Law, are a law to themselves, in that they show the work of the Law written in their hearts, their conscience bearing witness and their thoughts alternately accusing or else defending them, on the day when, according to my gospel, God will judge the secrets of men through Christ Jesus. '*

Everybody is born with a conscience. If you were born in a remote third world country, there are still customs, practices and perhaps tribal norms that guide morals and values. It might be OK in that culture to take another man's wife or steal his cow. However, it might be a violation of custom to insult the chief and you could be stoned for such behavior. It doesn't matter the specific of the values, the point Paul is making is that even Gentiles who do not have the written Ten Commandment Law, have a conscience and an unwritten law in their hearts that condemns them when they violate their conscience. That's why he concludes in Romans 3:23 that all (Jews and Gentiles) have all sinned. Once a person sins, they are in need of a Savior and as we've already seen, there is no other name given under heaven by which we may be saved and forgiven except Jesus. The Gospel is the only remedy for the sin of all humanity.

Is sprinkling a substitute for baptism?

The Greek word *baptidzo* means to dip, plunge under or submerge. The English word *baptize* if translated would say *Immerse*. *"Repent and be immersed for the forgiveness of sins."*

Here's an example of what Biblical baptism looks like. Phillip the evangelist was travelling on a desert road near Gaza when he encountered a chariot returning from Jerusalem headed back to Ethiopia. The passenger was the Treasury Secretary for the Queen of Ethiopia and being a wealthy man had his very rare copy of an Isaiah scroll. He was reading the section in chapter fifty three, "He was led as a sheep to the slaughter." Not understanding to whom this scripture referred he asks Phillip to explain it.

> *Acts 8:34-39*
>
> *'The eunuch answered Philip and said, "Please tell me, of whom does the prophet say this; of himself or of someone else?" Then Philip opened his mouth, and beginning from this Scripture he preached Jesus to him. As they went along the road they came to some water; and the eunuch said, "Look! Water! What prevents me from being baptized?" And Philip said, "If you believe with all your heart, you may." And he answered and said, "I believe that Jesus Christ is the Son of God." And he ordered the chariot to stop; and they both went down into the water, Philip as well as*

the eunuch, and he baptized Him. When <u>they came up out of the</u>
<u>water,</u> the Spirit of the Lord snatched Philip away; and the
eunuch no longer saw Him, but went on his way rejoicing. '

We can clearly see that being baptized required one to "go down into and come up out of" the water. It's a burial. Sprinkling and pouring are manmade substitutions that were introduced only after the erroneous teaching about original sin and infant baptism began.

Here's another side comment for your consideration on this passage. Some ask, "What if I'm in the desert and there's no water?" Well, when they came to some water, then he got baptized. Did you notice that Phillip was preaching to Him Jesus then his next question was about baptism? This shows that you can't preach the Gospel of Christ without including baptism because that's the Gospel Jesus commanded to be preached. "Go make disciples; baptizing them…"

Lots of churches baptize people for lots of different reasons. Most Calvinistic churches misread the Great Commission. The Great Commission says, "Go into all the world and preach the Gospel. "Whoever believes **and** is baptized shall be saved." Most teach it this way, "Whoever believes and invites Jesus into your heart is saved, and should be baptized to join the church, or as an outward sign of an inward grace." The problem is that it doesn't say that! Let me show you that you can't be taught wrong and then baptized right. There's only one baptism that God accepts and you must understand what you are doing and why.

> *Ephesians 4:4-5*
>
> *'There is one body and one Spirit, just as also you were called in one hope of your calling; one God and Father of all who is over all and through all and in all. <u>One Lord, one faith,</u> <u>one baptism</u>"*

Let me show you an account where a well-intentioned preacher didn't understand the difference between the baptism of John and the baptism of the New Covenant.

Acts 18:24-26

'Now a Jew named Apollos, an Alexandrian by birth, an eloquent man, came to Ephesus; and he was mighty in the Scriptures. This man had been instructed in the way of the Lord; and being fervent in spirit, <u>he was speaking and teaching accurately the things concerning Jesus, being acquainted only with the baptism of John</u>; and he began to speak out boldly in the synagogue. But when Priscilla and Aquila heard Him, they took him aside and explained to him the way of God more accurately. '

Apollos was speaking powerfully and accurately the things about Jesus, but apparently didn't get the memo that John's baptism was in force in the previous covenant. When Jesus died, the New Covenant went into force and therefore Johns' baptism was no longer valid. It was immersion, but its purpose was different and therefore didn't count any longer. Watch what happens:

Acts 19:1-5

'It happened that while Apollos was at Corinth, Paul passed through the upper country and came to Ephesus (where Apollos had been preaching) and found some disciples. He said to them, "Did you receive the Holy Spirit when you believed?" And they said to Him, "No, we have not even heard whether there is a Holy Spirit." And he said, "Into what then were you baptized?" And they said, "Into John's baptism." Paul said, "John baptized with the baptism of repentance, telling the people to believe in Him who was coming after Him, that is, in Jesus." When they heard this, they were baptized in the name of the Lord Jesus."

Remember back to Acts 2:38 where Peter said, "Repent and be baptized in the name of Jesus Christ for the forgiveness of sins and you will receive the gift of the Holy Spirit?" When Paul asked if they'd received the Holy Spirit and they had no clue what he was talking about. He immediately questioned their baptism. John's baptism was a baptism of repentance and pointing people to Jesus who would later come and be recognized as Messiah. When they heard what Paul said, then were re-baptized with the one baptism that was now part of the New Covenant.

At that point they had their sins washed away and forgiven, they received the Holy Spirit, they were united with and clothed in Christ and became heirs of the promise made to Abraham. You can't be taught wrong and baptized right. That's why I asked you to write down what you were taught in regard to your own conversion story on your life line.

There is now only one baptism that is required under the New Covenant. If you were baptized with another baptism that the Bible does not command, like sprinkling, pouring or immersion for the wrong reason like Johns' baptism, then you've been baptized incorrectly and I would highly recommend you get baptized immediately for the right reason. That's what I did when I discovered this truth.

> *John 3:3-5*
>
> *'Jesus answered and said to Him, "Truly, truly, I say to you, unless one is born again he cannot see the kingdom of God." Nicodemus said to Him, "How can a man be born when he is old? He cannot enter a second time into his mother's womb and be born, can he?" Jesus answered, "Truly, truly, I say to you, <u>unless one is born of water and the Spirit he cannot enter into the kingdom of God.</u>*
>
> *Titus 3:5*
>
> *'He saved us, not on the basis of deeds which we have done in righteousness, but according to His mercy, by the <u>washing of rebirth and renewing by the Holy Spirit"</u>*

This is exactly what Peter preached in the first Gospel Sermon ever preached on Pentecost in Acts 2. Repent and be baptized (Born of water) for the forgiveness of sins and you will receive the gift of the Holy Spirit.

What about the thief on the cross?

People have questions about the thief on the cross. He wasn't baptized. Well, there are some solid answers for you to consider. First, Jesus told Him that He would be in Paradise with Him that very day. Jesus has all authority in heaven and on earth, so when Jesus tells a person they're going to be in Paradise, then that's authority. He told the paralytic lowered through the roof, "In order to know that the Son of Man has authority on earth to forgive sins, I tell you take up your pallet and walk."

But there's another important truth for you to consider. When Jesus told the thief on the cross that message, Jesus hadn't died yet, therefore the New Covenant was not yet in force. New Covenant baptism is a reenactment of the death, burial and resurrection of Jesus. It would have been impossible for the thief to reenact Jesus' death, burial and resurrection since it hadn't happened yet and the New Covenant had not yet been activated.

So what does your life line look like? Does it show that you were sprinkled as an infant, then later you were "confirmed?" I hope you see that's incorrect. Did you make an altar call and invite Jesus into your heart or say the sinners' prayer, then may-be you got baptized a year or so later to join the church? Again, I hope you've learned from scripture that this is as incorrect as those baptized into Johns' baptism in Acts 19.

Why different people were told different things.
I've heard these questions a lot over the last forty three years. The Bible says that, "God so loved the world that whoever believes should not perish but have eternal live." The understanding from this is that all one has to do is believe in Jesus. We've already shown that even the devil believes so that's apparently not all one must do. We've also looked at Matthew 7:21-23 and what Jesus will say to many on the judgment day, "Not everyone who says to me 'Lord, Lord' will enter the kingdom of heaven, but only he who does the will of my Father in heaven." So believing and acknowledging Jesus as Lord won't cut it either!

When the jailer in Philippi asked Peter, "What must I do to be saved?" Peter answered, "Believe in the Lord Jesus and you will be saved, you and your household." (Acts 16:20-31).

And when the people asked Peter on the day of Pentecost, "Brothers, what shall we do?" Peter responded, "Repent and be baptized for the forgiveness of your sins and you will receive the gift of the Holy Spirit," (Acts 2:38). Then when Peter kept on pleading with them to save themselves it says, "Those who accepted his words were baptized and there were added that day about three thousand souls." So how do we understand this apparent discrepancy?

Let's say you were travelling from Seattle to Miami and asked someone how far it was. They would answer, "The distance is 3,321 miles." So you drive to Denver and ask the same question, "How far is it to Miami?" You would receive an answer, "The distance to Miami is 2,064 miles." If you continue on your journey and fuel your car in St. Louis, MO and ask, "How far is it to Miami? You would get an answer, "The distance to Miami is 1,215 miles!" You asked the same question, but received a different answer each time. Why? You received a different answer because you were at a different location in your journey.

The jailer had never heard of Jesus before, so when he asked, "What must I do?" Peter responded, "Believe in the Lord Jesus and you will be saved." Peter went to his home, taught him and his family and then he and his household were baptized that very night after midnight after hearing the rest of the story. Think about this, a jailer who could be executed for letting his prisoners escape takes his captives home to his family. Then in the middle of the night lets these prisoners take him and his family to the river and lets them hold them under water and baptizes them all. This wasn't some sacrament they all went to church to receive on "Baptism Sunday!" It was something urgent and life changing. "Whoever believes and is baptized will be saved," (Mark 16:15).

When the Jews on Pentecost heard Peter's reasoning about Jesus being the fulfillment of Old Testament prophecies and the son of David who would occupy his throne they believed that Jesus was in fact the Son of God and then asked, "What must we do (now that we believe)?" Peter said, "Repent and be baptized for the forgiveness of your sins and your will receive the gift of the Holy Spirit... Save yourselves... and those who received his word (to be saved) were baptized.. about three thousand of them." No altar all, no sinner's prayer. Repent and be baptized.

So where are you at in the journey? If you have never heard of Jesus like the jailer or like the Ethiopian on the road to Gaza, you first have to believe that Jesus is the Son of God and is raised from the dead. Once you believe then the next answer to your question is, "Repent and be baptized for the forgiveness of your sins! Save yourself! And when you respond, you, like the three thousand on Pentecost will be baptized to be clothed in Christ and have your sins washed away and receive the indwelling of the Holy Spirit.

Are you listening?
From this chapter we've learned that you must believe in Jesus, be willing to die to sin and self (repent), confess Jesus as your Lord, and be immersed in water as an obedient act of faith in the working of God to remove your sin, receive the gift of the Holy Spirit, and be put "In Christ." This is how you are Born Again (John 3:1-5). If you haven't obeyed God's will as revealed in the Bible, you are not yet saved. There is no mention of a sinner's prayer or inviting Jesus into your heart in any of these examples. There is only One Lord, One faith, and One Baptism that God commands and accepts (Ephesians 4:4-5). He will accept no substitutions.

The decision to accept Jesus' invitation is a serious one and you must count the cost of your commitment to become a disciple. The benefits are eternal life, forgiveness of all your sins, and peace with God. One hundred years from now, friends, family, and possessions will all be gone, however where you spend eternity will be fixed forever. Are you ready to be born again of the water and the Spirit? I've been praying for you, the reader, and hope you will follow faith's formula today.

God's command
+ trusting obedience put into action
= Faith that saves.

"Whoever believes AND is baptized will be saved!" (Mark 16:15)

The next step is up to you. Trust in Christ and be united with Him in baptism today. God bless you in your journey.

What kind of soil are you?

Matthew 13:3-9

Then He spoke many things to them in parables, saying: "Behold, a sower went out to sow. As he sowed, some seed fell by the wayside; and the birds came and devoured them. Some fell on stony places, where they did not have much earth; and they immediately sprang up because they had no depth of earth. But when the sun was up they were scorched, and because they had no root they withered away. And some fell among thorns and the thorns sprang up and choked them. But others fell on good ground and yielded a crop: some a hundredfold, some sixty, some thirty. He who has ears to hear, let him hear!"

What does this parable mean to you?

Matthew 13:18-23

"Therefore hear the parable of the sower: When anyone hears the word of the kingdom, and does not understand it, then the wicked one comes and snatches away what was sown in his heart. This is he who received seed by the wayside. But he who received the seed on stony places, this is he who hears the word and immediately receives it with joy; yet he has no root in himself, but endures only for a while. For when tribulation or persecution arises because of the word, immediately he stumbles. Now he who received seed among the thorns is he who hears the word, and the cares of this world and the deceitfulness of riches choke the word, and he becomes unfruitful. But he who received seed on the good ground is he who hears the word and understands it; who indeed bears fruit and produces: some a hundredfold, some sixty, some thirty."

This parable is challenging you to test the kind of heart you have and how receptive you are to the message of the Kingdom of God and God's offer of salvation to you. Some people hear the message and for some reason don't "Get it!" They don't understand their need for the offer of salvation. The devil has blinded their minds; they dismiss the message and go on their merry way. Is that you? I hope not.

Others hear it and accept the message with great eagerness; but then for whatever reason quit when they experience some criticism for their new-found faith in Christ. None of us likes to be criticized but when you follow Christ you need to expect it and if it bothers you, you won't stick. Is that you? Again, I hope not.

Others accept the message but then life happens and things get in the way. Bills pile up, the kids have troubles, you lose your job, or you become wildly successful and make a lot of money and you forget your commitment to Christ and put Him on the sidelines and it all goes away. Satan uses all kinds of tactics to divert your attention away from your eternity. Don't let that be you!

Remember Jesus said the gate is narrow that leads to life and only a few find it? These are the reasons. The few are those who accept the message of salvation, understand the commitment and hold on like a bull dog and endure whatever comes at them because they realize that a billion years from now it will be all worth it! Life's short; death's sure; judgment's final; and eternity is forever. Are you listening? I hope you are and I hope you graciously, humbly and tenaciously accept Gods' loving offer of eternal life.

My good friend Tim just died Sunday

As I was finalizing my book my good friend Tim Morrow died in a motel room from a stroke. I met Tim in 1990 when I moved back to Helena, Montana and he was my insurance agent. In our first conversation Tim said he'd love to learn more about the Bible and offered to train me in body-building if I'd teach him more about the Bible. I eagerly agreed. We started working out every morning and at lunch he would come to my office where I worked as a financial advisor and we'd go through the Bible and study the exact lessons you've been learning as you read this book. Tim was a really funny guy and 'ripped' muscle wise. In college he was a draft choice for the Dallas Cowboys and also the Chicago Bears as a wide receiver. He blew his knee out and that ended his NFL career.

I vividly remember the day I baptized Tim into Christ as you've learned in this book. That day was the real funeral of Tim Morrow. He died with Christ and when he came up out of the water he was born again, a new man in Christ and had eternal life and was now indwelled with the Holy Spirit.

He couldn't stop talking about his new-found salvation in Christ. He told everybody he knew. Some thought, "Ol Tim was a little crazy," and his family criticized him, but he kept on sharing what he'd found. Eventually his mom Adeline and his dad Ed were baptized one night after we studied with them over their kitchen table; again with the same lessons you've just read. Tim brought a lot of people to Christ and I could tell you story after story of the lives that were changed for eternity because he was fruitful in his relationship with God.

Tim's health took a turn for the worst about two years ago with a simple bladder infection that damaged his liver, kidneys and his heart was only working at 12%. I talked to Tim just last Saturday about 2 pm and he was really weak and hired some help to load his U-Haul so he could move his stuff back to Helena, Montana and then pull his trailer to Las Vegas for the winter. He stopped at a motel and a clot in his leg broke loose and gave him a stroke and he died in his sleep. We have been very close friends for twenty eight years and upon hearing of his death I haven't shed a single tear. I know where my brother is and I have total confidence that one billion years from now we'll be sharing eternity together because we both accepted the Good News. How about you?

I hope you realize the value of what you've learned in this book. The mystery of eternal life has now been unveiled for you. What kind of soil are you. I hope you have the kind of heart my friend Tim did. I hope to see you a billion years from now! See you in eternity!

Chapter 6 - The New Testament Church

What is the church? Today if you look through your yellow pages you'll see a variety of churches with different creeds, traditions and teachings. Is there really a difference between the church in the Bible and the churches of today? Which church did Paul start when he went into a new city? When you read through the Book of Acts; you'll learn how the church began in Acts 2 then you'll observe Paul travelling throughout the Roman Empire establishing churches in different cities on three separate missionary journeys. He wasn't establishing different denominations; rather he was establishing the same church that Jesus promised to establish.

But can we be like the church in the Bible today and if so, how? In this chapter we will examine what the New Testament teaches concerning God's church and how to identify it and be a part of it today.

I. Who Built the Church

Peter's Confession of Christ

Matthew 16:13-18

Now when Jesus came into the district of Caesarea Philippi, He was asking His disciples, "Who do people say that the Son of Man is?" And they said, "Some say John the Baptist; and others, Elijah; but still others, Jeremiah, or one of the prophets." He said to them, "But who do you say that I am?" Simon Peter answered, "You are the Christ, the Son of the living God." And Jesus said to him, "Blessed are you, Simon Barjona, because flesh and blood did not reveal this to you, but My Father who is in heaven. I also say to you that you are Peter, and upon this rock I will build My church; and the gates of Hades will not overpower it. I will give you the keys of the kingdom of heaven; and whatever you bind on earth shall have been bound in heaven, and whatever you loose on earth shall have been loosed in heaven.

Jesus had been with His apostles almost three years by this time and He wanted to test their understanding of who He was. They never comprehended that Jesus was God in the flesh or that He was the Creator of the Universe and they were still unclear about His identity as the Messiah or Christ that was predicted in all the Old Testament passages. They were expecting that He might be the promised King of the Jews who would overturn the Romans and establish a political kingdom like in the glory days of King David. Their understanding was still unclear until they received the Holy Spirit on the day of Pentecost; but more about that later in the book.

Who do men say I am? Some supposed Jesus might be a resurrected John the Baptist or Elijah or one of the other prophets from the Old Testament. No one quite comprehended His identity. Now Jesus asks the apostles who *they* think He is. Peter jumped in with a bold declaration, "You are the Christ, the Son of the Living God!" This confession is the basis for Jesus' next declaration, "I say you are Peter *(petros {masculine gender in Greek meaning pebble}) and upon this Rock (petra {feminine gender in Greek meaning bedrock foundation}) I will build my Church."* Jesus said that it was upon the foundation of Peters' confession that He was the Christ that He would build His church. The church was not build on Peter but upon Jesus being the Christ – the promised Messiah.

Peter was given the keys to the kingdom; which is the church and when using the *keys;* Peter's sermons opened the entry to the kingdom when he preached the first Gospel sermon to the Jews in Acts 2 and the first Gentiles to be included in Christ in Acts 10.

When Paul talked of planting churches and teaching the Gospel, he said this:

1 Corinthians 3:10-11

According to the grace of God which was given to me, like a wise master builder I laid a foundation, and another is building on it. But each man must be careful how he builds on it. <u>For no man can lay a foundation other than the one which is laid, which is Jesus Christ.</u>

We must understand that the church is Jesus' idea; not mans'. The church was built upon Christ as the Chief Cornerstone and it belongs to Him and Him alone. He alone is the head of His church which is also called "the body of Christ."

Colossians 1:18

He is also head of the body, the church; and He is the beginning, the firstborn from the dead, so that He Himself will come to have first place in everything.

Remember that in the first century when the church started in AD 33 in Jerusalem on the day of Pentecost, every disciple of Jesus was a member of the same church. There were no denominations or sects until later on in the late first and second centuries. Just as there is only one Lord, one God, one faith, one baptism, even so there is only one body or church of which Jesus is Head.

Ephesians 4:4-5

There is one body and one Spirit, just as also you were called in one hope of your calling; one Lord, one faith, one baptism, one God and Father of all who is over all and through all and in all.

Ephesians 1:22-23

And He put all things in subjection under His feet, and gave Him as head over all things to the church, which is His body, the fullness of Him who fills all in all.

Before His betrayal, Jesus prays to the Father that all His followers be one. He knew division and controversy would arise after His departure. He warned that a house divided against itself cannot stand (Matthew 12:25).

John 17:20-21

"I do not ask on behalf of these alone, but for those also who believe in Me through their word; that they may all be one; even as You, Father, are in Me and I in You, that they also may be in Us, so that the world may believe that You sent Me.

It wasn't long after the church began to see the beginning of divisions; some the result of doctrinal misunderstanding; some the result of personalities. Some believers felt very strongly that before a Gentile could become a member of the church he must first be circumcised and convert to Judaism. This was an extremely strong controversy that prompted the writing of the book to the Galatian churches and a Jewish council meeting with the Apostles in Jerusalem.

In the Corinthian church we see evidence of believers gravitating to certain personalities and their teaching style rather than to Christ alone. The immaturity of these newer believers seems to have prompted them to brag about who taught or baptized them. People can be passionate about their favorite sports team or athlete; but it's not supposed to be this way in the Household of God. Here's Paul's response:

1 Corinthians 1:10-13

Now I exhort you, brethren, by the name of our Lord Jesus Christ, that you all agree and that there be no divisions among you, but that you be made complete in the same mind and in the same judgment. For I have been informed concerning you, my brethren, by Chloe's people, that there are quarrels among you. Now I mean this, that each one of you is saying, "I am of Paul," and "I of Apollos," and "I of Cephas," and "I of Christ." Has Christ been divided? Paul was not crucified for you, was he? Or were you baptized in the name of Paul? I thank God that I baptized none of you except Crispus and Gaius, so that no one would say you were baptized in my name."

We witness this same tendency throughout history when believers identify themselves with prominent teachers such as Luther or Calvin or identifying themselves with a certain practice like baptism after which the Anabaptist and Baptist churches were named. It's understandable why people do this, but Paul said it's wrong and it's exactly what Jesus prayed would not occur. Religious division is wrong. It was Jesus who purchased His church and His name alone should identify believers. Paul planted a church in the city of Ephesus and established elders or shepherds in each church he planted. Notice his strong admonition to these elders as he warns them that men will come from among their own members as savage wolves to draw believers away after themselves. They are to be on guard to shepherd the church of God which He purchased with His own blood.

> Acts 20:28-30
>
> *Be on guard for yourselves and for all the flock, among which the Holy Spirit has made you overseers, to shepherd the church of God which He purchased with His own blood. I know that after my departure savage wolves will come in among you, not sparing the flock; and from among your own selves men will arise, speaking perverse things, to draw away the disciples after them.*

What was the church called and how were believers identified in the first century? A church was typically identified by the city in which it existed – i.e."*The church of God in Corinth.*" It was called the Church of God 8 times (ie. 1 Corinthians 1:2); the Church of the firstborn ones (Hebrews 12:23); the churches of Christ - 1 time (Romans16:16); The Way - 5 times (ie. Acts 9:2-5); the body - 2 times (Ephesians 1:23); Family of God (1 Peter 4:17); House of God, Household of God and Household of faith (Ephesians 2:19; Galatians 6:10; Hebrews 10:21); Temple of the Living God (2 Corinthians 6:16); City of the Living God, Heavenly Jerusalem; Mount Zion (Hebrews 12:22); The Israel of God (Galatians 6:16).

Members of the church were called disciples; saints (sanctified ones) - 61 times; members of one another, Christians -3 times; a royal priesthood, living stones (1 Peter 2:5), believers – 53 times; the called; the chosen; brothers or brethren - 113 times.

When one looks at the New Testament, the reference to the church and believers always gave glory to God and His holiness and identifies people as part of an eternal family designed and purchased by God. The church and her believers never gave glory to a man's name or a religious practice. Shouldn't it be that way today?

II. Traditions of Men vs. the Word of God

Jesus warned of the danger of implementing and following traditions when it comes to religious practices. His strongest condemnations and scolding tones are aimed not at sinners, but at the religious elite who started traditions and bound them on others as a requirement to be right with God. One wouldn't think that washing hands could be a big deal; and any good mom is going to require her kids to wash their hands before they eat. This is not the same as the religious tradition of washing hands that made it a sin and a standard by which a person's orthodoxy could be judged. Jesus condemned that type of tradition.

The Pharisees had another tradition that violated one of the Ten Commandments to honor your father and mother. The word *honor* is a financial term that meant it was the children's responsibility to take care of mom and dad especially in their old age when they needed financial support. The Pharisees changed that and said, "Well, yes you're supposed to help mom and dad, but let's make your giving to the synagogue more important. After all, wouldn't you rather give to God than your parents? It's more holy to do it that way." Churches throughout history have fallen prey to the deceitfulness of similar practices. Let's examine a couple of examples of what those traditions look like and the warnings Jesus issues.

> *Matthew 15:1-14*
>
> *Then some Pharisees and scribes came to Jesus from Jerusalem and said, "Why do Your disciples break the tradition of the elders? For they do not wash their hands when they eat bread." And He answered and said to them, "Why do you yourselves transgress the commandment of God for the sake of your tradition? For God said, 'HONOR YOUR FATHER AND MOTHER,'*

and, 'HE WHO SPEAKS EVIL OF FATHER OR MOTHER IS TO BE PUT TO DEATH.' But you say, 'Whoever says to his father or mother, "Whatever I have that would help you has been given to God," he is not to honor his father or his mother.' And by this you invalidated the word of God for the sake of your tradition. You hypocrites, rightly did Isaiah prophesy of you:

'THIS PEOPLE HONOR ME WITH THEIR LIPS, BUT THEIR HEART IS FAR AWAY FROM ME. 'BUT IN VAIN DO THEY WORSHIP ME, TEACHING AS DOCTRINES THE PRECEPTS OF MEN.'"

After Jesus called the crowd to Him, He said to them, "Hear and understand. It is not what enters into the mouth that defiles the man, but what proceeds out of the mouth, this defiles the man."

Then the disciples came and said to Him, "Do You know that the Pharisees were offended when they heard this statement?" But He answered and said, "Every plant which My heavenly Father did not plant shall be uprooted. Let them alone; they are blind guides of the blind. And if a blind man guides a blind man, both will fall into a pit."

So you can see from Jesus' encounter with the Pharisees that He was irate at the idea of man-made traditions that either changed the clear teaching of God such as honoring your parents or even washing hands as evidence of your religious orthodoxy. He said that people who follow those types of traditions would be pulled up by the roots and they worship God in vain! The apostles were shocked and advised Jesus to tone it down a bit, but He firmly renounced those man-made traditions.

Let's examine another section where Jesus rejected the wearing of religious type clothes and religious titles that exalt men as superior religiously.

Matthew 23:1-10

Then Jesus spoke to the crowds and to His disciples, saying: "The scribes and the Pharisees have seated themselves in the chair of Moses; therefore all that they tell you, do and observe, but do not do according to their deeds; for they say things and do not *do them. They tie up heavy burdens and lay them on men's shoulders, but they themselves are unwilling to move them with so much as a finger. <u>But they do all their deeds to be noticed by men; for they broaden their phylacteries and lengthen the tassels of their garments. They love the place of honor at banquets and the chief seats in the synagogues, and respectful greetings in the market places, and being called Rabbi by men. But do not be called Rabbi; for One is your Teacher, and you are all brothers. Do not call anyone on earth your father; for One is your Father, He who is in heaven. Do not be called leaders; for One is your Leader, that is, Christ.</u> But the greatest among you shall be your servant. Whoever exalts himself shall be humbled; and whoever humbles himself shall be exalted.*

Are you catching the nature of what's happening here? You had religious leaders who made themselves superior as "clergy" above the average person in the community. They did this by the garments they wore and the titles they assigned to themselves.

Phylacteries were leather pouches containing scripture that they would wear sometimes on their foreheads as a sign of how religious they were. "If my phylactery is bigger than yours, then I'm more religious because I have more verses memorized." They would wrap a prayer shawl over their shoulders and when they prayed they would braid the tassels on the end. The longer my tassels, the more prayers I said which showed how holy I am compared to you. They also assigned to themselves religious titles like Rabbi or Father and by so doing their religious authority was made superior and they received special honor and recognition in public gatherings.

I'm sure by now you're seeing how these traditions have been implemented in many churches. Men give themselves titles like *Father, Reverend, Pastor, His Most Holy Excellence, Pope, Cardinal,* and a myriad of other names and titles which is exactly what Jesus said not to do. You see clergy wearing robes and collars or strange golden hats and ornaments and have people bow down to kiss their ring. You can be assured that Jesus would issue the same condemnation and scolding rebuke to those traditions today as He did in the first century and He would say that those who follow those traditions worship God in vain.

Now I need to clarify here that there were leadership ministries in the early church with designations like Elder, Deacon, Evangelist, but these are not the same as the self-exalting titles and clergy-laity role you see in churches today. Let's briefly look at some of those leadership ministries.

III. Leadership Ministries

The first leadership ministry we'll see is that of an elder or in the KJV it translates it as bishop, pastor or shepherd. The Greek words *presbuteros, episkopos and pastoras* all refer to the same ministry. These men were the God-appointed overseers and shepherds of each congregation and were entrusted with the ministry to guide, teach and care for the members of the congregation and to ensure the church stayed faithful to the teachings and practices of Jesus. Paul and Barnabas visited churches they had planted on the first missionary journey and upon their return they appointed elders in each church.

> *Acts 14:23*
>
> *When they had appointed elders for them in every church, having prayed with fasting, they commended them to the Lord in whom they had believed*
>
> *. Acts 20:17, 28-30*
>
> *From Miletus he sent to Ephesus and called to him the elders of the church. Be on guard for yourselves and for all the flock, among which the Holy Spirit has made you overseers, to shepherd the church of God which He purchased with His own blood. I know that after my departure savage wolves will come in among you, not sparing the flock; and from among your own selves men will arise, speaking perverse things, to draw away the disciples after them. Therefore be on the alert, remembering that night and day for a period of three years I did not cease to admonish each one with tears.*

The books of Timothy and Titus are called *Pastoral Epistles or Letters.* Timothy and Titus were evangelists, not pastors, but the instruction for appointing pastor/elders is given in these books; thus the name *Pastoral Epistles.* Let's examine what is taught in these letters about the character and qualities required for men to be elder/pastor/overseers.

Titus 1:5-9

For this reason I left you in Crete, that you would set in order what remains and appoint elders in every city as I directed you, namely, if any man is above reproach, the husband of one wife, having children who believe, not accused of dissipation or rebellion. For the overseer must be above reproach as God's steward, not self-willed, not quick-tempered, not addicted to wine, not pugnacious, not fond of sordid gain, but hospitable, loving what is good, sensible, just, devout, self-controlled, holding fast the faithful word which is in accordance with the teaching, so that he will be able both to exhort in sound doctrine and to refute those who contradict.

For there are many rebellious men, empty talkers and deceivers, especially those of the circumcision, who must be silenced because they are upsetting whole families, teaching things they should not teach for the sake of sordid gain. One of themselves, a prophet of their own, said, "Cretans are always liars, evil beasts, and lazy gluttons." This testimony is true. For this reason reprove them severely so that they may be sound in the faith, not paying attention to Jewish myths and commandments of men who turn away from the truth.

Here we have another glimpse into the ministry of elders. They must be married men with believing children and live lives that are exemplary of the Christian life of integrity and holiness. Their ministry again is identified as exhorting the church in sound doctrine and refuting those who contradict. In the following section from Timothy we see these men are called overseers in the NASB and bishops in the KJV. It's the same Greek word.

1Timothy 3:1-7

It is a trustworthy statement: if any man aspires to the office of overseer, it is a fine work he desires to do. An overseer, then, must be above reproach, the husband of one wife, temperate, prudent, respectable, hospitable, able to teach, not addicted to wine or pugnacious, but gentle, peaceable, free from the love of money. He must be one who manages his own household well, keeping his children under control with all dignity (but if a man does not know how to manage his own household, how will he take care of the church of God?), and not a new convert, so that he will not become conceited and fall into the condemnation incurred by the devil. And he must have a good reputation with those outside the church, so that he will not fall into reproach and the snare of the devil.

So what about those churches that have bishops who are required to be single in order to be clergy? Sounds like a violation of the Word of God; doesn't it? Just a slight diversion here so you'll see what the Bible says about this practice.

2 Timothy 4:1-3

But the Spirit explicitly says that in later times <u>some will fall away from the faith, paying attention to deceitful spirits and doctrines of demons</u>, by means of the <u>hypocrisy of liars</u> seared in their own conscience as with a branding iron, <u>men who forbid marriage and advocate abstaining from foods</u> which God has created to be gratefully shared in by those who believe and know the truth

The Bible calls those who forbid marriage and advocate abstinence from certain foods on certain days as a religious practice *Deceitful Spirits and Doctrines of Demons and Hypocrisy of Liars.* This practice is a *falling away from the faith* that was established by the Holy Spirit in the Word of God.

A second ministry mentioned in the New Testament is that of *Deacon*; which was a ministry that seems to serve the physical needs of members of the church (1Timothy 3:8-12; Philippians 1:1). An example of the type of ministry they might be leading is the feeding of the Grecian Widows in the church who were being overlooked in the daily distribution of food in Acts 6. Phoebe is a woman mentioned by Paul in Romans 16:1-2 as a deaconess (diakonon) and a helper of many.

A third ministry was that of an Evangelist (2 Timothy 4:5; Acts 21:8). Timothy was told to do the work of an evangelist. This is what would be thought of as a preacher, or one who proclaims the Good News. You can read through the books of First and Second Timothy and Titus to see a full description of the work of an evangelist; one of which was to appoint elders in each church and to admonish the believers to adhere to sound teaching.

IV. The Worship of the Church

As followers of Christ, worship is a central expression of our love, honor, respect and adoration of God. If you want to see the heart-felt expression of a man after God's own heart you can look at the life and writings of King David by reading through the Psalms. It's a recommended habit to read a chapter in Proverbs each day and two to three chapters in Psalms.

Psalms are a collection of songs; some of which were sung in the temple worship; others were sung in private worship as David expressed his cries to God for deliverance from his enemies or questioning God's intensions or even songs of repentance and cries for forgiveness for his own sin. If you want to draw close in your emotions to God there is really no better way than to read Psalms.

God is seeking true worshippers whose desire it is to honor and praise Him. God's not on an ego trip by any means, but is an expression of praise from the Creature to his Creator.

> *John 4:24*
>
> *But an hour is coming, and now is, when the true worshipers will worship the Father in spirit and truth; for such people the Father*

seeks to be His worshipers. God is spirit and those who worship Him must worship in spirit and truth."

Matthew 22:36-38

Teacher, what is the great commandment in the Law?" And He said to him, "you shall love the Lord your God with all your heart, and with all your soul, and with all your mind.' This is the great and foremost commandment.

We've already looked at the vain worship of man-made traditions. Worship in spirit deals with attitude and the heart and truth is that which is genuine and according to the Word of God. Think about it this way. When I want to get my wife a gift that means something very special to her; I'll often ask her and she'll tell me. She'll tell me the color and size and even the brand that she wants. Now if I'm smart, I'll get her what she wants because it's my desire to please her and demonstrate my love for her. It's the same with God. He tells us certain items of worship that being honor and pleasure as our Father in Heaven. Let's look at a few examples.

Romans 12:1-2

Therefore I urge you, brethren, by the mercies of God, to present your bodies a living and holy sacrifice, acceptable to God, which is your spiritual service of worship. And do not be conformed to this world, but be transformed by the renewing of your mind, so that you may prove what the will of God is, that which is good and acceptable and perfect.

Paul mentioned in 1 Corinthians 6 that a reason to abstain from sexual immorality is that our body is the temple of the Holy Spirit and that the Spirit dwells in is. We are not our own, we've been bought at a price, therefore honor God with our body. When we respect our body sexually and keep ourselves from conforming to the world by renewing our minds, it proves what the will of God is. It is a spiritual service in our worship that is good, acceptable and perfect.

Personal holiness is one of the most honoring acts of worship we offer to our God and Father through Jesus Christ. But there are some other items the early church did in their times of fellowship together. They recognized Sunday as the Lord's Day, or first day of the week and it became the day believers typically gathered for special worship and fellowship. This was the day Jesus was raised from the dead.

We learn from Acts 2 what some of the lifestyle was in the church and what their lives were like.

Acts 2:42-47

They were continually devoting themselves to the apostles' teaching and to fellowship, to the breaking of bread and to prayer.

Everyone kept feeling a sense of awe; and many wonders and signs were taking place through the apostles. And all those who had believed were together and had all things in common; and they began selling their property and possessions and were sharing them with all, as anyone might have need. Day by day continuing with one mind in the temple, and breaking bread from house to house, they were taking their meals together with gladness and sincerity of heart, praising God and having favor with all the people. And the Lord was adding to their number day by day those who were being saved.

The early church was devoted to one another and love was a characteristic for which they were known even by skeptics on the outside. One early author accused them of sexual immorality and cannibalism because they witnessed their love for each other and they shared the Lord's Supper. In Acts 2 pilgrims had travelled from all over the Empire to gather for a 50 day celebration of Passover and Pentecost and those who accepted the Gospel stayed longer due to their new-found faith in Christ. People were selling their possessions and sharing with each other gladly and sincerely in the new church and people were coming to Christ daily and being saved. How exciting that must have been.

As mentioned above, taking the Lord's Supper was something the early church did and it was often part of a pot luck dinner. A problem occurred in the church in Corinth and it appears some of the believers were forgetting that this was to be a family gathering so they would hurry up and eat before the less fortunate saints arrived. Paul reminds them of the purpose of the Supper and instructs them that this is a matter of love, fellowship and caring for our other brethren in a loving manner and waiting for them.

1 Corinthians 11:23-29

For I received from the Lord that which I also delivered to you, that the Lord Jesus in the night in which He was betrayed took bread; and when He had given thanks, He broke it and said, "This is My body, which is for you; do this in remembrance of Me."In the same way He took the cup also after supper, saying, "This cup is the new covenant in My blood; do this, as often as you drink it, in remembrance of Me." For as often as you eat this bread and drink the cup, you proclaim the Lord's death until He comes. Therefore whoever eats the bread or drinks the cup of the Lord in an unworthy manner, shall be guilty of the body and the blood of the Lord. But a man must examine himself, and in so doing he is to eat of the bread and drink of the cup. For he who eats and drinks, eats and drinks judgment to himself if he does not judge the body rightly.

From Acts 20:7 and also extra biblical writings it appears they shared Communion weekly; a message was delivered by one of the men; usually an elder; they sang praises sometimes from the Psalms (Ephesians 5:19; Colossians 3:16) and took care of one another's needs.

Sometimes they would meet publicly in the temple square in Jerusalem but most of their church life was spent in each other's homes (Acts 20:20). Even in the church in Colossae, special greeting is given in the letter to Philemon to Apphia our sister and Archippus and the church that meets in his home (Philemon 1:1-2).

There was a famine in the church in Palestine and a famine relief ministry was conducted by Paul to bring funds from the churches around the Mediterranean back to Jerusalem (1 Corinthians 16:1-2; 2

Corinthians 8-9). This shows that the early church gave financially to take care of other churches and also supported Paul and others in their preaching ministries. Jesus taught about giving to the poor in Matthew 6 and stressed the importance of doing it with genuineness and not to be seen just to attract praise to yourself. A tragic occurrence happens in Acts 5 to a couple named Ananias and Sapphira. Members of the church were selling property and real estate and bringing the proceeds to the apostles for distribution to those in need. This couple for some sad reason decided to lie about their contribution and they both dropped dead because they lied to the Holy Spirit.

V. The Mission and Message of the Church

Church life in the first century was very grass root in nature. Someone said Christianity was born in a cave and died in a Cathedral. The more "formal" Christian services became the more tradition took over and it seems like the further away from the culture of the early church it grew. Today most churches in the West resemble an educational model rather than a mission-driven model. "Faithfulness" is measured by how many times one shows up when the church doors are open rather than looking at the fruitfulness of one's life and ministry to others. With that model, the typical Western church has stagnated and makes little impact in its culture as salt and light and little evangelism occurs.

So what did Jesus say was the mission of the church?

> *Matthew 28:18-20*
>
> *And Jesus came up and spoke to them, saying, "All authority has been given to Me in heaven and on earth. Go therefore and make disciples of all the nations, baptizing them in the name of the Father and the Son and the Holy Spirit,0teaching them to observe all that I commanded you; and lo, I am with you always, even to the end of the age."*

The mission of the church is the salvation of the world by carrying out what is called The Great Commission. God commissioned His church to make disciples.

Mark 16:15-16

And He said to them, "Go into all the world and preach the gospel to all creation. He who has believed and has been baptized shall be saved; but he who has disbelieved shall be condemned

So what is your part in carrying out the Great Commission? When is the last time you shared your faith in Christ with a friend, family, co-worker or neighbor? It's our mission to the world!

VI. The Purpose of the Church

Ephesians 1:9-11

He made known to us the mystery of His will, according to His kind intention which <u>He purposed</u> in Him with a view to an administration suitable to the fullness of the times, that is, the summing up of all things in Christ, things in the heavens and things on the earth. In Him also we have obtained an inheritance, having been predestined according to His purpose who works all things after the counsel of His will,

The purpose of the church is to bring all things together under one head – Christ, and in that process; the church brings glory to God. The entire Bible and the establishment of the church is all about the salvation of people back to their creator – God our Father through the Gospel of Christ.

Ephesians 2:14-16

For He Himself is our peace, who made both groups (Jew and Gentile) into one and broke down the barrier of the dividing wall, by abolishing in His flesh the enmity, which is the Law of commandments contained in ordinances, so that in Himself He might <u>make the two into one new man, thus establishing peace,</u> and might reconcile them both in one body (the church) to God through the cross, by it having put to death the enmity.

The purpose of the church is to reconcile people back together into the Family of God by being clothed in Christ. (Galatians 3:26-29). When the angels and beings in the heavenly realm see how God is saving and reuniting people back together in the church, it declares God's incredible wisdom to the whole universe. (Ephesians 3:10-11). The church is a big deal in God's eternal purpose!

VII. God's purpose for YOU in the church

Ephesians 5:23-27

For the husband is the head of the wife, as Christ also is the head of the church, He Himself being the Savior of the body. But as the church is subject to Christ, so also the wives ought to be to their husbands in everything.

Husbands, love your wives, just as Christ also loved the church and gave Himself up for her, so that He might sanctify her, having cleansed her by the washing of water with the word, that He might present to Himself the church in all her glory, having no spot or wrinkle or any such thing; but that she would be holy and blameless.

Jesus is the head of the church which is His bride. He loves the church and gave Himself up for her to sanctify or make her holy and present her to Himself in all her glory. Some people try to say "Jesus – yes; the church – no!" But you can't tell Jesus you love Him if you don't love his bride. When you're added to Christ in baptism, he adds you to the church and you now have a family.

As family in Christ, there is a level of commitment we are to have for one another. You are part of a body and have a ministry given by God.

1 John 3:16

We know love by this; that He laid down His life for us; and we ought to lay down our lives for the brethren.

1 Corinthians 12:12-25

For even as the body is one and yet has many members, and all the members of the body, though they are many, are one body, so also is Christ. For by one Spirit we were all baptized into one body, whether Jews or Greeks, whether slaves or free, and we were all made to drink of one Spirit.

For the body is not one member, but many. If the foot says, "Because I am not a hand, I am not a part of the body," it is not for this reason any the less a part of the body. And if the ear says, "Because I am not an eye, I am not a part of the body," it is not for this reason any the less a part of the body. If the whole body were an eye, where would the hearing be? If the whole were hearing, where would the sense of smell be? But now God has placed the members, each one of them, in the body, just as He desired. If they were all one member, where would the body be? But now there are many members, but one body. And the eye cannot say to the hand, "I have no need of you"; or again the head to the feet, "I have no need of you." On the contrary, it is much truer that the members of the body which seem to be weaker are necessary; and those members of the body which we deem less honorable, on these we bestow more abundant honor, and our less presentable members become much more presentable, whereas our more presentable members have no need of it. But God has so composed the body, giving more abundant honor to that member which lacked, so that there may be no division in the body, but that the members may have the same care for one another.

The church is like a body and each of us is a different part of that body. Some are eyes, hands, feet and some are little toes. If you stub your toe your whole body reacts. Regardless of what part you are; you are valuable and important.

Attendance and commitment to a group of other believers in a Bible based church or small group is important to your spiritual development.

Hebrews 10:23-25

Let us hold fast the confession of our hope without wavering, for He who promised is faithful; and let us consider how to stimulate one another to love and good deeds, not forsaking our own assembling together, as is the habit of some, but encouraging one another; and all the more as you see the day drawing near.

The Jewish believers were looking in anticipation to the destruction of Jerusalem that Jesus predicted in Matthew 24. As they saw the day approaching they were encouraged to hold fast the confession of their hope without wavering and needed to stimulate one another to love and good works (Hebrews 10:25). You can't live a fruitful Christian life by yourself. God never designed it that way; so He established the church as a family to support you and others.

Why you need to be committed to your church family:
1. It identifies you as a genuine believer (John 13:34).
2. It moves you out of self centered isolation (1 John 3:16).
3. It helps you develop spiritual muscle (Ephesians 4:16).
4. You have a mutual responsibility to others in God's family (1 Corinthians 12:27).
5. You get to share in Christ's mission in the world. (Ephesians 2:10).
6. It helps keep you from backsliding (Hebrews 3:13).

VIII. Conclusion

Ephesians 2:19

So then you are no longer strangers and aliens, but you are fellow citizens with the saints, and are of God's household,

Now that you are a believer united with Christ make sure you plug into a healthy church where you can grow and mature in Christ. You need the fellowship and others need your fellowship in their lives. The church was established and purchased by Christ. Ready to plug in and get to work?

We've seen that the church is the kingdom of God but now we need to examine some teaching about the Kingdom and the reign of Christ. Again we're gonna kick the cage around the zoo and challenge some common misconceptions about the Kingdom.

Chapter 7 -The Kingdom of God vs. Millennial Mania

The kingdom of God has long been the topic of discussion among religious people. The Jews in Jesus' day questioned Him about the coming of the kingdom and His response made little sense to them. Some today teach that Jesus did not set up His kingdom the first time He was here because the Jews rejected Him and so He had to come up with another plan to set up the Church as an after-thought; a kind of audible on the line of scrimmage. Many now teach that He is coming again to set up His earthly kingdom in Jerusalem and will reign there on the Throne of David for 1,000 years. This is referred to as the Millennial Reign of Christ and is derived from Revelation 20.

You hear about all the "Signs of the times" – earthquakes; rumors of war; unrest in the Middle East; etc. We're warned that the 'Time is near.' Look at the Middle East… Jesus is coming soon! People are migrating to Israel and hope to be there when Jesus returns on the Mount of Olives to set His earthly kingdom in Jerusalem. At that time the Temple will be rebuilt; and the Roman Empire will re-emerge.

There is a book series that has been super popular, "Left Behind," that talk about all the sinners who will be left behind at the Rapture. You hear horror stories of airplanes being flown by Christian Pilots that are "raptured" and the plan is flying without a pilot and all the sinners are in horror because their pilot is immediately 'Beamed Up.' This will be followed by the great tribulation. There are some who believe in "Pre-Tribulation" and others who are "Post-Tribulation." The doctrine is very confusing and even those who hold to the basics of it don't agree how it's all supposed to happen. To their credit, even the Christians in Thessalonica misunderstood the second coming of Christ and thought

141

they might have missed it. But is any of this really true? I used to believe a lot of this teaching until I started looking at what the Bible actually said and discovered most of what I'd learned was not true; just like the "Pray Jesus into your heart" teaching. It's just not in the Bible!

We're gonna kick the cage around the zoo again on this topic as well, so hold onto your seat. You're about to learn a whole new way of thinking after you see what the Bible really says in regard to the topic of the Kingdom of God. In this chapter we will examine what the Old Testament prophets said in reference to the kingdom and then we will see what Jesus said in reference to the subject.

Three End-Time Events
There are actually three "End-Time Events" that are taught in the New Testament:

1. The destruction of Jerusalem (Matthew 24:1-34; Luke 21).
2. The fall of the Roman Empire (Revelation 1-20).
3. The second coming of Jesus and the end of the world (1 Thessalonians 4:13-18; 2 Peter 3).

The confusion happens because people mix them all together instead of looking at the context. I'm not going to go into great detail about these three end time events, but just a few comments for you to consider.

First, concerning the destruction of Jerusalem that occurred in 70 AD. Jesus gave signs to look for; rumors of wars, earthquakes etc. and told people to flee to the mountains of Judea (Matthew 24 and Luke 21). They were to hope that it didn't occur in the winter or on the Sabbath because the gates to the city would be closed. When they saw the city surrounded by the abomination that causes desolation as prophesied by Daniel 9 they were not to hesitate, but escape immediately lest one be taken and the other left behind.

Second, the destruction of Rome is the overwhelming theme of the book of Revelation. Rome was devouring the Christians, especially the seven churches in Asia Minor. They were encouraged to endure to the end because God would surely avenge the Great Harlot sitting on the beast that was drinking the blood of the saints. *"The woman you saw is the great city that rules over the kings of the earth," (Revelation 17:18) and the seven heads of the beast are 7 hills upon which the city sits," (17:9).* There are seven hills surrounding the city of Rome. *"Woe! Woe to you, great city, you mighty city of Babylon! In one hour your doom has come!" (Revelation 18:10).* The Great beast is the same beast we see in Daniel 7:7 which scholars agree is the Roman Empire.

Third, the second coming of Jesus and the end of the world will be the "Last Day" of earth. Notice how the second coming of Christ and the end of the world is vastly different than the predictions of the destruction of Jerusalem:

- The second coming of Christ will be the "Last Day." *For my Father's will is that everyone who looks to the Son and believes in him shall have eternal life, and I will raise them up at **the last day**," (John 6:40).* This Last Day is when Jesus descends with a loud shout and the voice of the Archangel and the dead in Christ will be raised first them we who are alive will be caught up with them in the air (1 Thessalonians 4:13-18). Jesus said that at that same hour, both the righteous and unrighteous will be raised from the dead, *"Do not be amazed at this, for a time is coming when all who are in their graves will hear his voice and come out—those who have done what is good will rise to live, and those who have done what is evil will rise to be condemned" (John 5:28-29).*
- The second coming will be the end of the world with nowhere to escape. There will be no running to the hills of Judea! And unlike the signs warning of the destruction of Jerusalem, the second coming of Jesus will have no warning. He will come like a thief! *"But the day of the Lord will come like a thief. The heavens will disappear with a roar; the elements will be destroyed by fire, and the earth and everything done in it will be laid bare...That day will bring about the destruction of the heavens by fire, and the elements will melt in the heat," (2 Peter 3: 10-12).* At the

destruction of Jerusalem, the days "were cut short" but when Christ returns all the dead will be raised in one instant, the universe destroyed, the judgment happens and a new heaven and new earth will be created.

OK, enough of the three end-time events discussion for now, but hope this gives you something to study further. Do you have your seat buckled to have your thoughts challenged? Get your pen, underline some stuff and open your heart to take an honest look at what the Bible actually teaches about the Kingdom of God... and it's not what you might think and it's not what others are telling you!

I. Old Testament Prophesies about the Kingdom of God

Isaiah 2:1-3

The word which Isaiah the son of Amoz saw <u>concerning Judah and Jerusalem</u>. Now it will come about that <u>In the last days The mountain of the house of the LORD Will be established as the chief of the mountains</u>, And will be raised above the hills; And <u>all the nations will stream to it.</u> And many peoples will come and say, "Come, let us go up to the mountain of the LORD, To the house of the God of Jacob; That He may teach us concerning His ways And that we may walk in His paths." <u>For the law will go forth from Zion And the word of the LORD from Jerusalem</u>.

The Jewish concept was that a glorious kingdom would be restored like in the days of Solomon. Isaiah is talking about the kingdom of God being established and gives some very specific identifiers.
- First the prophecy is concerning Judah and Jerusalem.
- Second, the kingdom would include all nations or ethnic groups, not only Jews.
- Third, the kingdom would be called "The Mountain of the Lord" and "The House of God."
- Fourth, the kingdom would be established in "The Last Days."
- Fifth, the word of the Lord would go forth from Jerusalem.

We'll show from the New Testament where these specifics are already fulfilled.

In the following verses found in Daniel we will see that the Kingdom of God was prophesied to be established in the time of the Roman Empire. Israel was in Babylonian captivity that started in the year 606 BC and ended in 586 BC seventy years later. Nebuchadnezzar was the king of Babylon and had a terrifying dream about a large statue with four parts which represented four kingdoms. Daniel, a young Jewish captive, was summoned to interpret the dream for the king. Here is the dream and its interpretation.

> *Daniel 2:31-45*
>
> *You, O king, were looking and behold, there was a single great statue; that statue, which was large and of extraordinary splendor, was standing in front of you, and its appearance was awesome. The head of that statue was made of fine gold, its breast and its arms of silver, its belly and its thighs of bronze, its legs of iron, its feet partly of iron and partly of clay. You continued looking until a stone was cut out without hands, and it struck the statue on its feet of iron and clay and crushed them. Then the iron, the clay, the bronze, the silver and the gold were crushed all at the same time and became like chaff from the summer threshing floors; and the wind carried them away so that not a trace of them was found. But the stone that struck the statue became a great mountain and filled the whole earth.*
>
> ### The Interpretation-Babylon the First Kingdom
>
> *"This was the dream; now we will tell its interpretation before the king. You, O king, are the king of kings, to whom the God of heaven has given the kingdom, the power, the strength and the glory; and wherever the sons of men dwell, or the beasts of the field, or the birds of the sky, He has given them into your hand and has caused you to rule over them all.* **You are the head of gold.**

Medo-Persia and Greece

After you there will arise another kingdom inferior to you, then another third kingdom of bronze, which will rule over all the earth.

Rome

Then there will be a fourth kingdom as strong as iron; inasmuch as iron crushes and shatters all things, so, like iron that breaks in pieces, it will crush and break all these in pieces. in that you saw the feet and toes, partly of potter's clay and partly of iron, it will be a divided kingdom; but it will have in it the toughness of iron, inasmuch as you saw the iron mixed with common clay. As the toes of the feet were partly of iron and partly of pottery, so some of the kingdom will be strong and part of it will be brittle. And in that you saw the iron mixed with common clay, they will combine with one another in the seed of men; but they will not adhere to one another, even as iron does not combine with pottery.

The Divine Kingdom

In the days of those kings (the kings of the fourth world kingdom – Rome) the God of heaven will set up a kingdom which will never be destroyed, and that kingdom will not be left for another people; it will crush and put an end to all these kingdoms, but it will itself endure forever. Inasmuch as you saw that a stone was cut out of the mountain without hands and that it crushed the iron, the bronze, the clay, the silver and the gold, the great God has made known to the king what will take place in the future; so the dream is true and its interpretation is trustworthy."

As you've just read, Daniel interpreted the kings' dream and told him that the statue represented four world kingdoms, the first of which was Babylon. The second kingdom historically that overthrew Babylon was Medo-Persia (586 BC – 331 BC). The Greeks overthrew the Persians and established the Grecian Empire (331 BC – 63 BC). The fourth kingdom that overthrew the Greeks was Rome (63 BC – about 400 AD).

<u>Daniel clearly stated that in the days of the kings of the fourth world empire (Rome), the God of heaven would set up a kingdom that would never be destroyed.</u>

Later, Daniel himself has a vision about this same kingdom that would be established. One like a Son of Man (Christ) was to <u>ascend</u> into the presence of The Ancient of Days (God) and at that time he was given dominion, glory and a kingdom and men from every nation and language might serve him. His kingdom would be an everlasting dominion and would not be destroyed.

> *Daniel 7:13-14*
>
> *"I kept looking in the night visions, And behold, with the clouds of heaven One like a Son of Man was coming, and He came up to the Ancient of Days (God the Father). And was presented before Him and to Him was given dominion, Glory and a kingdom that all the peoples, nations and men of every language might serve Him.*
>
> *His dominion is an everlasting dominion which will not pass away; and His kingdom is one which will not be destroyed.*

So, let's look carefully at what is being prophesied here. The prophets say that the kingdom of God would begin in the fourth world kingdom, the Roman Empire. The Son of Man (Christ), must *ascend* and be presented to the Ancient of Days (God) in order to receive this kingdom. The word of the Lord would go forth from Jerusalem and all nations (ethnic groups) would be drawn to and included in this kingdom.

II. The New Testament Promise of the Kingdom

The Jewish nation had long awaited the fulfillment of the Old Testament promises concerning the establishment of the kingdom of God. From reading their own scripture they were longing in eager anticipation for a new ruler who would overthrow the Roman pagans and once-again return Israel to her previous glory like in the days of Solomon. John the Baptist was the forerunner to Christ and I want you to notice what his first message was to Israel. The kingdom that you've been expecting from Isaiah and Daniel is about to be established!

Matthew 3:1-2

Now in those days John the Baptist came, preaching in the wilderness of Judea, saying, "Repent, for the kingdom of heaven is at hand.

Then when Jesus starts his ministry, He proclaims the same message. The long awaited kingdom is about to emerge; so get ready.

Matthew 4:17

From that time Jesus began to preach and say, "Repent, for the kingdom of heaven is at hand."

But how soon was this kingdom to appear? Would it take another two thousand or so years to be established? No. It would be established in the lifetime of those to whom Jesus was speaking.

Mark 9:1

And Jesus was saying to them, "Truly I say to you, there are some of those who are standing here who will not taste death until they see the kingdom of God after it has come with power."

Two indications were given by Jesus as to the coming of the kingdom of God. 1) It would come in the lifetime of those listening and 2) it would come with power. We'll see when that exactly happened. But what would this kingdom be like? Would it be a military overthrow of the Romans? No. Would it be a political kingdom with borders, armies and world domination? No. Look at its character in the following verses.

Luke 17:20-21

Now having been questioned by the Pharisees as to when the kingdom of God was coming, He answered them and said, "The kingdom of God is not coming with signs to be observed; nor will they say, 'Look, here it is!' or, 'There it is!' For behold, the kingdom of God is in your midst." (or is within you).

So Jesus contrasts the kingdom of God with all other worldly kingdoms. You can't point to it on a map or measure its territory. The kingdom of God of which Jesus speaks would be a spiritual kingdom within the hearts of those who submitted to Jesus as King.

In another passage Jesus is being interrogated about the nature of His kingdom. "Are you a king?" Jesus replied, "Yes, but my kingdom is not of this world. If it were, I would have an army who would not let their king be captured." The kingdom of God is much different than what the Jews and the Romans were expecting.

> *John 18:36*
>
> *Jesus said, "My kingdom is not of this world. If it were, my servants would fight to prevent my arrest by the Jewish leaders. But now my kingdom is from another place."*

I want you to notice a conversation Jesus is having with Peter. This is where we get all the jokes about Peter standing at the pearly gates but it's not what Jesus is talking about. Christ is telling Peter that He would build His church and then tells him in the same sentence that He would give him the keys to the kingdom. Keys were the standards for entry into the kingdom, which is the church Jesus established.

> *Matthew 16:18-19*
>
> *Jesus replied, "Blessed are you, Simon son of Jonah, for this was not revealed to you by flesh and blood, but by my Father in heaven. And I tell you that you are Peter, and on this rock (The fact that I am the Christ) I will build my church, and the gates of Hades will not overcome it .I will give you the keys of the kingdom of heaven; whatever you bind on earth shall have been bound in heaven, and whatever you loose on earth shall have been loosed in heaven.*

Jesus didn't change subjects here when talking to Peter. He told Peter that upon the fact that I am the Christ, I will give you the keys to the kingdom and by inspiration of the Holy Spirit you will proclaim the parameters of entry into My kingdom. If you recall from our early conversation, Peter's sermon on Pentecost was the first time the keys to the kingdom were used to unlock entry when he preached the Gospel and three thousand were baptized into Christ and added to the kingdom of God.

Luke 24:44-49

He said to them, "This is what I told you while I was still with you: Everything must be fulfilled that is written about me in the Law of Moses, the Prophets and the Psalms."

Then he opened their minds so they could understand the Scriptures. He told them, "This is what is written: The Messiah will suffer and rise from the dead on the third day, and repentance for the forgiveness of sins will be preached in his name to all nations, beginning at Jerusalem. You are witnesses of these things. I am going to send you what my Father has promised; but stay in the city until you have been clothed with power from on high."

Jesus reminded His apostles that everything written about Him in the Old Testament must be fulfilled, including His death, burial and resurrection. Remember, they didn't comprehend any of this even though He told them plainly. Repentance and forgiveness of sins – the word of the Lord – would be preached to all nations beginning at Jerusalem. They were to stay in the city until they had been clothed with power from on high.

OK, quick review here. Daniel and Isaiah's prophecies about Jesus and His kingdom must be fulfilled and it was about to happen. Remember Isaiah 2:3 – the word would be preached from Jerusalem? Jesus just reconfirmed that. Remember Mark 9:1, the kingdom would come with power? Jesus just reminded them that they were about to receive that power and the kingdom was about to be established in the lifetime of those to whom Jesus preached and this was in the Roman Empire. Everything is coming together. You ready for more? I hoped you'd say yes. Let's continue!

The day of Pentecost arrives and thousands of pilgrims were gathered in Jerusalem for the most historical event in history; though they never expected it. Watch closely what happens and pay attention to the predictions we've already talked about. Jesus tells His apostles to stay in Jerusalem and they would receive power; and they did!

Acts 1:8; 2:1-4

But you will receive power when the Holy Spirit comes on you; and you will be my witnesses in Jerusalem, and in all Judea and Samaria, and to the ends of the earth." After he said this, he was taken up before their very eyes, and a cloud hid him from their sight. **(Jesus ascended back to the Father and here receives the kingdom as predicted in Daniel 7:13-14).**

When the day of Pentecost came, they were all together in one place. Suddenly a sound like the blowing of a violent wind came from heaven and filled the whole house where they were sitting. They saw what seemed to be tongues of fire that separated and came to rest on each of them. All of them were filled with the Holy Spirit and began to speak in other tongues as the Spirit enabled them.

So the apostles received the power they had been promised and the kingdom of God had now been established. We'll explain more of the details as we explore some of the following verses.

Acts 2:16-17

This is what was spoken by the prophet Joel: 'In the last days, God says, I will pour out my Spirit on all people. Your sons and daughters will prophesy, your young men will see visions, your old men will dream dreams. Even on my servants, both men and women, I will pour out my Spirit in those days,

If you remember, Isaiah 2 and Joel 2 said that the kingdom would be established in the 'last days.' Peter just confirmed that what the people were witnessing was the fulfillment of Joel's prophecy – this was 'the last days.' This also was in Jerusalem as Isaiah prophesied and as Daniel 2:44 so clearly predicted. This was in the days of the fourth world kingdom, the Roman Empire. But the question many people ask and are confused about is this, "Is Jesus on the Throne of David as the Old

Testament clearly predicted?" The answer is yes, but it's not on earth and that's where the confusion arises. Let's examine this more closely.

> *Luke 1:31-33*
>
> *You will conceive and give birth to a son, and you are to call him Jesus. He will be great and will be called the Son of the Most High. <u>The Lord God will give him the throne of his father David,</u> and he will reign over Jacob's descendants forever; <u>his kingdom will never end.</u>"*

Mary was told by the angel that her Son Jesus would be given David's throne as promised in the prophets and His kingdom would never end. Peter in his sermon on Pentecost addresses this promise and shows when it was fulfilled.

> *Acts 2:29-36*
>
> *"Brethren, I may confidently say to you regarding the patriarch David that he both died and was buried, and his tomb is with us to this day. And so, because <u>he was a prophet and knew that God had sworn to him with an oath to seat one of his descendants on his throne, he looked ahead and spoke of the resurrection of the Christ,</u> that he was neither abandoned to Hades, nor did His flesh suffer decay. This Jesus God raised up again, to which we are all witnesses. <u>Therefore having been exalted to the right hand of God,</u> and having received from the Father the promise of the Holy Spirit, He has poured forth this which you both see and hear.*
>
> *For it was not David who ascended into heaven, but he himself says: 'the Lord said to my Lord, "<u>sit at my right hand,</u> until I make your enemies a footstool for your feet."' Therefore let all the house of Israel know for certain that <u>God has made Him both Lord and Christ-this Jesus whom you crucified.</u>"*

WOW, there you have it! Mary was reminded that her Son was THE descendant that was promised David's throne. Peter reminds the crowd that David was a prophet and knew that God had sworn to him with an oath to seat one of his descendants on his throne. BUT what was David talking about when he made this statement? Did you catch it? Peter said he was actually referring to the resurrection and ascension of Jesus. He is NOW Lord and Christ (meaning anointed ruler).

Remember Daniel 7:13-14 when one like the Son of Man would *ascend* before the Ancient of Days and given a kingdom? Peter just clarified that when he said, "Therefore having been exalted to the right hand of God." It wasn't David who ascended into heaven, it was Jesus who ascended and sat down at the right hand of God and was crowned as King of Kings and Lord of Lords and is now seated upon David's throne as prophet, priest and king and has all authority in heaven and earth as ruler over the kingdom of God. Check out these verses and you'll see its true!

> *Hebrews 1:3*
>
> *And He is the radiance of His glory and the exact representation of His nature, and upholds all things by the word of His power. When He had made purification of sins, He sat down at the right hand of the Majesty on high*

> *Hebrews 8:1*
>
> *Now the main point in what has been said is this: we have such a high priest, who has taken His seat at the right hand of the throne of the Majesty in the heavens*

Jesus IS already seated on the throne of David, therefore the kingdom of God has been established! Those who are in Christ are part of that kingdom as Paul explains in the following verse.

> *Colossians 1:13*
>
> *For He rescued us from the domain of darkness, and transferred us to the kingdom of His beloved Son, in whom we have redemption, the forgiveness of sins.*

The Hebrew writer is showing the magnificence of what Jesus did and reminding us what we're part of in Hebrews 12. I want you to remember what you read in Isaiah, Joel, Daniel and Acts and you'll see that what was promised concerning the kingdom of God is already a reality. The rule of Christ reigning on the throne of David is expressed in wonderful terms – Mount Zion, the city of the living God, the heavenly Jerusalem, the church of the firstborn who are enrolled in heaven and the kingdom which cannot be shaken. If you're in Christ, you are in the kingdom of God that was promised centuries ago. Jesus is already in His "thousand year reign!"

Hebrews 12:22-23, 28

But you have come to <u>Mount Zion</u> and to <u>the city of the living God, the heavenly Jerusalem,</u> and to myriads of angels, to the general assembly and <u>church of the firstborn who are enrolled in heaven,</u> and to God, the Judge of all, and to the spirits of the righteous made perfect, and to Jesus, the mediator of a new covenant, and to the sprinkled blood, which speaks better than the blood of Abel.

Therefore, <u>since we receive a kingdom which cannot be shaken,</u> let us show gratitude, by which we may offer to God an acceptable service with reverence and awe.

I want to remind you how you see the kingdom of God and how you enter it. Do you remember what Jesus said to Nicodemus? Let's read it again.

John 3:1-7

*Now there was a man of the Pharisees, named Nicodemus, a ruler of the Jews; this man came to Jesus by night and said to Him, "Rabbi, we know that You have come from God as a teacher; for no one can do these signs that You do unless God is with him." Jesus answered and said to him, "Truly, truly, I say to you, <u>unless one is born again **he cannot see** the kingdom of God."</u>*

*Nicodemus said to Him, "How can a man be born when he is old? He cannot enter a second time into his mother's womb and be born, can he?" Jesus answered, "Truly, truly, I say to you<u>, unless one is born of water and the Spirit **he cannot enter** into the kingdom of God</u>*

When you accept God's terms of pardon in Christ and are born again of water and spirit, then you can *SEE* and you can *ENTER* the kingdom of God, which is the church of the living God, Mount Zion, and the heavenly Jerusalem. Peter, when using the keys of the kingdom for the first time mentioned these two elements of the new birth; water and spirit.

> *Acts 2:38*
>
> *Peter said to them, "Repent, and each of you be baptized (Water) in the name of Jesus Christ for the forgiveness of your sins; and you will receive the gift of the Holy Spirit (Spirit) = born again = part of the kingdom of God!*

Why the reign of Christ on earth is impossible

I used to believe the teaching about the thousand year reign of Christ on earth and looked with anticipation for its occurrence. However, the more I examined scripture; I came to the conclusion that this doctrine is false and has many serious consequences that many of my friends who believe in it have not considered. Let me share with you some of those.

1. Christ cannot reign on earth

After the death of Jehoiakim, king of Judah, Jehoiachin, his son, reigned in his place as king of Judah in 597 BC (2 Kings 24:5,6; Jeremiah 22:22:24-30.). Jehoiachin had reigned only three months when Nebuchadnezzar's army came and took him and his family into captivity (2 Kings 24:8-10). With reference to Jehoiachin, Jeremiah writes:

> *Jeremiah 22:30*
>
> *For no more shall a man of his seed prosper sitting upon the throne of David and ruling in Judah.*

Jehoiachin was of the seed of David and it was through his lineage that Christ was born (Matthew 1:12). He had children, but not one of these sons reigned as king of Judah in Jerusalem for Jeremiah clearly prophesied that was never again going to happen.

So, since Jesus is a descendant of Jehoiachin who is a descendant of David, it's very clear that Jesus can NEVER reign on David's throne from Jerusalem in Judah. There is no possible way for Him to reign on earth in Judah and be in harmony with the prophecy of Jeremiah 22:30!

2. Christ cannot be a priest on earth

Zechariah prophesied that the Messiah would be both priest and king at the same time. "And he shall sit and rule upon his throne," (Zech 6:13). The Hebrew writer reaffirms that Jesus, since He is not from the tribe of Levi (the priestly tribe) could never be a priest while on earth.

> *Hebrews 8:4*
>
> *Now the main point in what has been said is this: <u>we have such a high priest, who has taken His seat at the right hand of the throne of the Majesty</u> **in the heavens,** a minister in the sanctuary and <u>in the true tabernacle</u>, which the Lord pitched, not man. For every high priest is appointed to offer both gifts and sacrifices; so it is necessary that this high priest also have something to offer. **<u>Now if He were on earth, He would not be a priest at all</u>**

Did you catch that? If Jesus has to come back to earth to sit on the earthly throne of David, then He MUST abandon His ministry as High Priest because He cannot be a priest at all on earth which means that we would no longer have an intercessor who offers Himself as our supreme sacrifice. Are you seeing the dilemma here?

Christ cannot sit on a literal throne of David in Judah because Jeremiah 22:30 said there will never again be a king on the throne of David reigning from Judah. However, Jesus is both High Priest and King, ruling from His Throne in heaven and ministering as High Priest for the forgiveness of our sins. Neither of which can occur if He ever comes back to earth!

If He comes back to earth to reign for one thousand years He violates the prophecies that state clearly that no one from Jehoiachin can ever rule on David's throne in Judah and He must forfeit His Priesthood because He is forbidden from being a priest on earth!

3. He must descend to receive His kingdom

Daniel 7:13-14 clearly states that the Son of Man must ASCEND and come into the presence of the Ancient of Days to receive His kingdom. However, the millennial view mandates that Jesus descend from heaven to come back to earth to receive His kingdom. Jesus ascended in Acts 1 and went into the presence of the Ancient of Days and Peter emphatically testified that He sat on David's Throne as Lord and Christ in doing so. The term *Christ* means He IS the ruling King right now!

The entire "thousand year of Christ's Reign on earth" is fatally flawed when examined in light of scripture. This shows how dangerous it is to build an entire doctrine on apocalyptic literature, symbols and visions rather than on black and white scripture that give clear instruction.

In Revelation John opens the book with some wild visions.

> *Revelation 1:12-16*
>
> *Then I turned to see the voice that was speaking with me. And having turned I saw seven golden lamp stands; and in the middle of the lamp stands I saw one like a son of man, clothed in a robe reaching to the feet, and girded across His chest with a golden sash. His head and His hair were white like white wool, like snow; and His eyes were like a flame of fire. His feet were like burnished bronze, when it has been made to glow in a furnace, and His voice was like the sound of many waters. In His right hand He held seven stars, and out of His mouth came a sharp two-edged sword; and His face was like the sun shining in its strength.*

He clarifies what the seven stars and lamp stands are:

> *As for the mystery of the seven stars which you saw in My right hand, and the seven golden lamp stands: the seven stars are the angels of the seven churches, and the seven lamp stands are the seven churches.*

What do we learn from this? When symbols, or terms are used in apocalyptic literature, you cannot take them literally. You must base your interpretation upon clearly stated scripture that are not symbolic. We are presently in the thousand year reign of Christ and the kingdom of God has been established two thousand years ago.

III. Conclusion

The kingdom of God that the prophets saw and that John the Baptist and Jesus said was near was established in the lifetime of those who heard Jesus speak (Mark 9:1). Jesus received the kingdom when he ascended back to heaven after offering himself as a sacrifice for sin just as Daniel foretold (Daniel 7:13-14). When David spoke of one of his descendants sitting on his throne; Peter said he was speaking of the resurrection and ascension of Christ (Acts 2:29-36). The kingdom began in the last days in Jerusalem during the reign of the Roman Empire and included all nations as the prophets predicted. When the kingdom came, the word of the Lord was preached from Jerusalem and spread to the entire world.

Christ is presently reigning from His throne over His kingdom. When a person becomes a Christian, he is added to the kingdom of Christ (Colossians 1:13), which is the church of Christ; the heavenly Jerusalem, Mount Zion (Hebrews 12). The terms of entry into this kingdom are a birth of water and spirit (John 3:3-5). The kingdom is not of this world (John 18:36) and is therefore not visible or measurable as a political and military force (Luke 17:20-21).

Those who say that Jesus did not set up His kingdom yet have dethroned Jesus and called Him a liar (Mark 9:1), and have discredited the prophets that predicted that the kingdom would come in the days of the Roman Empire in the last days in Jerusalem. All these prophecies were fulfilled in Acts 2 on the day of Pentecost AD 33.

Chapter 8 – The Holy Spirit

The Holy Spirit is one of the personalities of the Godhead. He is Deity. Much confusion and misunderstanding has occurred over the past two centuries regarding the Holy Spirit, the Baptism of the Holy Spirit, the indwelling of the Spirit, and the miraculous manifestations of the Holy Spirit.

In this chapter we will consider the Biblical teaching about the Holy Spirit and see that there are three separate manifestations of the Spirit: the indwelling, the Baptism of the Spirit, and miraculous manifestations. We will look specifically at the miraculous manifestations in the next chapter.

Who is the Holy Spirit?

I. The Holy Spirit is a person

When we say that the Holy Spirit is a person; we in no way infer that He is a human being. He is one of the persons of the trinity – Father, Son and Holy Spirit. This is a much bigger topic than we will cover completely in this book; so I'd recommend you hunt down a copy of a classic book *The Timeless Trinity* by Roy Lanier Sr. But for now, let's uncover some verses to help you understand the third person of the Godhead – the Holy Spirit.

The Holy Spirit Has Emotion

> *Ephesians 4:30*
>
> *Do not grieve the Holy Spirit by whom you have been sealed for the day of redemption.*

We learn from this passage that we can grieve the Holy Spirit. From our context in Ephesians 4 we do this when we live contrary to the teachings of the Spirit in the Word of God. When we live in anger, steal, or let unwholesome words spring from our mouth; then we hurt the heart of the Holy Spirit and grieve Him.

> *Hebrews 10:28*
>
> *How much more severe punishment do you think he will deserve who has trampled underfoot the Son of God, and has regarded as unclean the blood of the covenant by which he was sanctified, and has <u>insulted the Spirit of grace?</u>*

We can insult the Holy Spirit by continually and deliberately sinning willfully and not appreciating the grace that was so free given to us.

> *Matthew 12:31-32*
>
> *Therefore I say to you, any sin and blasphemy shall be forgiven people, but <u>blasphemy against the Spirit shall not be forgiven.</u> Whoever speaks a word against the Son of Man, it shall be forgiven him; but whoever speaks against the Holy Spirit, it shall not be forgiven him, either in this age or in the age to come.*

The Holy Spirit can be blasphemed or spoken against in a false manner. The context of this verse is that people were witnessing Jesus perform undeniable miracles and crediting them to Satan and in essence, calling the Holy Spirit the Devil. As we'll learn later in the book; there certainly are counterfeit miracles that we need to discern; however to claim Jesus Himself was doing miracles by the power of Satan is unforgiveable.

> *Acts 7:51*
>
> *You men who are stiff-necked and uncircumcised in heart and ears <u>are always resisting the Holy Spirit</u>; you are doing just as your fathers did.*

In the context of this verse the Jews were resisting the preaching of Stephen the evangelist and were doing just as their fathers in the Old Testament did when they rejected the prophets God sent them.

The actions of the Holy Spirit are those of a person.

- The Holy Spirit Speaks

  1 Timothy 4:1

  But the Spirit explicitly says that in later times some will fall away from the faith, paying attention to deceitful spirits and doctrines of demons

- The Holy Spirit Hears

  John 16:13

  But when He, the Spirit of truth, comes, He will guide you into all the truth; for He will not speak on His own initiative, but whatever He hears, He will speak; and He will disclose to you what is to come.

- The Holy Spirit wills or determines

  1 Corinthians 12:11

  But one and the same Spirit works all these things, distributing to each one individually just as He wills.

- The Holy Spirit directs and chooses

  Acts 15:28; 16:7

  For it seemed good to the Holy Spirit and to us to lay upon you no greater burden than these essentials:

  They passed through the Phrygian and Galatian region, having been forbidden by the Holy Spirit to speak the word in Asia; 7and after they came to Mysia, they were trying to go into Bithynia, and the Spirit of Jesus did not permit them

- The Holy Spirit searches and knows

  1 Corinthians 2:10-11

  For to us God revealed them through the Spirit; for the Spirit searches all things, even the depths of God. For who among men knows the thoughts of a man except the spirit of the man which is in him? Even so the thoughts of God no one knows except the Spirit of God

- The Holy Spirit teaches

John 14:26

But the Helper, the Holy Spirit, whom the Father will send in My name, He will teach you all things, and bring to your remembrance all that I said to you

- The Holy Spirit intercedes

Romans 8:26-27

In the same way the Spirit also helps our weakness; for we do not know how to pray as we should, but the Spirit Himself intercedes for us with groanings too deep for words; and He who searches the hearts knows what the mind of the Spirit is, because He intercedes for the saints according to the will of God.

- The Holy Spirit guides

John 16:13

But when He, the Spirit of truth, comes, He will guide you into all the truth; for He will not speak on His own initiative, but whatever He hears, He will speak; and He will disclose to you what is to come

II. The Holy Spirit Is divine

- The Holy Spirit is everywhere (Omnipresent).

Psalms 139 7-10

Where can I go from Your Spirit? Or where can I flee from Your presence?

If I ascend to heaven, You are there; If I make my bed in Sheol, behold, You are there.

If I take the wings of the dawn, If I dwell in the remotest part of the sea, Even there Your hand will lead me,

And Your right hand will lay hold of me.

- The Holy Spirit is powerful (Omnipotent)

Romans 15:19

in the <u>power of the Spirit</u>; so that from Jerusalem and round about as far as Illyricum I have fully preached the gospel of Christ.

- The Holy Spirit knows the mind of God (Omniscient)

1 Corinthians 2:10-11

For to us God revealed them through the Spirit; for the Spirit searches all things, even the depths of God. For who among men knows the thoughts of a man except the spirit of the man which is in him? <u>Even so the thoughts of God no one knows except the Spirit of God.</u>

- The Holy Spirit is eternal

Hebrews 9:14H

How much more will the blood of Christ, <u>who through the eternal Spirit</u> offered Himself without blemish to God, cleanse your conscience from dead works to serve the living God?

- The Holy Spirit was active in the creation

Genesis 1:1-2

In the beginning God created the heavens and the earth. The earth was formless and void, and darkness was over the surface of the deep, and <u>the Spirit of God was moving over the surface of the waters</u>

- The Holy Spirit is one of the three persons of the Godhead

Matthew 28:19

And Jesus came up and spoke to them, saying, "All authority has been given to Me in heaven and on earth. Go therefore and make disciples of all the nations, baptizing them in the name of the <u>Father and the Son and the Holy Spirit</u>

When discussing the creation of man in the image of God, the Bible uses the plural "US"

> *Genesis 1:26*
>
> *Then God said, "Let Us make man in Our image.*

III. There are three manifestations of the Holy Spirit

- The Indwelling of the Holy Spirit
- The Baptism of the Holy Spirit
- The Miraculous gifts of the Holy Spirit

When you carefully examine the teaching about the Holy Spirit and how He reacts with humans it seems obvious that there are three separate and distinct manifestations of how He works. We will explore in this chapter the indwelling of the Holy Spirit which is a gift given to everyone who is baptized into Christ and receives the forgiveness of sins. We will also examine the Baptism of the Holy Spirit and see that this occurrence is recorded as happening only two times in the New Testament – Acts 2 upon the apostles and Acts 10 – upon Cornelius and his household.

The indwelling of the Holy Spirit

When Peter preached his sermon on the day of Pentecost the people were cut to the heart and asked Peter and the other apostles, "What shall we do," (Acts 2:37). Peter responded, "Repent and let each of you be baptized in the name of Jesus Christ for the forgiveness of your sins and <u>you will receive the gift of the Holy Spirit</u>," (Acts 2:38). This meant that the moment their sins were forgiven, the Holy Spirit Himself would be given as a gift to every individual and would literally take up residence in the body of those who were now saved.

> *Acts 5:32*
>
> *And we are witnesses of these things; and so is <u>the Holy Spirit, whom God has given to those who obey Him.</u>"*

Romans 8:9-11

However, you are not in the flesh but in the Spirit, <u>if indeed the Spirit of God dwells in you. But if anyone does not have the Spirit of Christ, he does not belong to Him</u>. If Christ is in you, though the body is dead because of sin, yet the spirit is alive because of righteousness. But <u>if the Spirit of Him who raised Jesus from the dead dwells in you, He who raised Christ Jesus from the dead will also give life to your mortal bodies through His Spirit who dwells in you.</u>

Paul references the fact that the Holy Spirit dwells in our mortal body as the motive for sexual purity.

1 Corinthians 6:18-20

Flee immorality. Every other sin that a man commits is outside the body, but the immoral man sins against his own body. Or do you not know that your body is a temple of the Holy Spirit who is in you, whom you have from God, and that you are not your own? For you have been bought with a price; therefore glorify God in your body.

The purpose for the indwelling of the Holy Spirit

Paul tells us that the indwelling of the Holy Spirit is a down-payment or seal that guarantees our inheritance. One version uses the term *Surety* or *Ernest* which is a financial term typically used in Real Estate transactions. If you make an offer to purchase a home, you sign an offer to purchase and attach a non-refundable deposit with that offer. If you back out of the offer to purchase; you forfeit your Ernest money. God gives us the gift of the Holy Spirit as an Ernest deposit guaranteeing that the remainder of our inheritance and salvation will be forthcoming or He forfeits the Holy Spirit – which cannot happen. This demonstrates that God's promise to save us is guaranteed! He can't back out!

Ephesians 1:13-14

In Him you also trusted, after you heard the word of truth, the gospel of your salvation; in whom also, having believed, you were sealed with the Holy Spirit of promise, who is the guarantee

*(Ernest – KJV) of our inheritance until the redemption of the
purchased possession, to the praise of His glory.*

The Holy Spirit also empowers the believer to put into action the
expectations of God in one's life.

Ephesians 3:16

*...that He would grant you, according to the riches of His glory, to
be strengthened with power through His Spirit in the inner man*

Have you ever struggled how to pray? For instance, if you have a faithful
believer in Christ who is seriously ill; do you ask God to take them home
or pray for a full recovery? Sometimes you can feel so hurt or
bewildered with issues in life you want to just throw up your hands in
frustration because you don't know how to pray or what to say. Don't
worry; the Holy Spirit communicates our inward groans to the Father
when we can't put words to our emotions. And, if you're a believer He
will cause all things to work together for good according to the will of
God.

Romans 8:26-28

*In the same way the Spirit also helps our weakness; for we do not
know how to pray as we should, but the Spirit Himself intercedes
for us with groanings too deep for words; and He who searches
the hearts knows what the mind of the Spirit is, because He
intercedes for the saints according to the will of God. And we
know that God causes all things to work together for good to
those who love God, to those who are called according
to His purpose*

The indwelling of the Holy Spirit is given to every believer upon being
baptized into Christ

Acts 2:38

*Repent and be baptized every one of you for the forgiveness of
sins and you will receive the gift of the Holy Spirit.*

John 3:5

Jesus answered, "Truly, truly, I say to you, unless one is born of water and the Spirit he cannot enter into the kingdom of God.

The Baptism of (or in) the Holy Spirit

Before Jesus ascended back to heaven, the Holy Spirit had never been given on earth in its full measure. Jesus told the apostles that it was necessary for Him to leave because if He didn't, the Spirit would not come; but if He left, He would send the Holy Spirit (John 16:7). We looked at this previously and the Holy Spirit finally came on the day of Pentecost.

We'll examine some of the characteristics of the coming of the Holy Spirit and observe that the Baptism of the Holy Spirit was received only by the apostles in Acts 2 and this miraculous event was so dynamic and rare that it never occurred again for ten years. When Cornelius and his household were baptized in the Holy Spirit; Peter explained that this was the same thing that happened to them ten years previously which indicates that it hadn't occurred since. We can assume that the apostle Paul was also baptized with the Holy Spirit possibly during his three years in Arabia when he was caught up into the third heaven; but we have no record of it (2 Corinthians 12:2; Galatians 1:15 ff.).

The baptism of the Holy Spirit was not a command but rather a promise

Acts 1:4-5

Gathering them together, He commanded them not to leave Jerusalem, but to wait for what the Father had promised, "Which," He said, "you heard of from Me; for John baptized with water, but you will be baptized with the Holy Spirit not many days from now."

The Outpouring of the Holy Spirit, which included the baptism of the Spirit and the Indwelling of the Spirit, was predicted by Joel the prophet. On the day of Pentecost, Peter clearly proclaims that what was occurring was the fulfillment of Joel's prophecy.

Joel 2:28-32

The Promise of the Spirit

"It will come about after this, that I will pour out My Spirit on all mankind; and your sons and daughters will prophecy, your old men will dream dreams; your young men will see visions. Even on the male and female servants I will pour out My Spirit in those days.

The Day of the Lord

"I will display wonders in the sky and on the earth; Blood, fire and columns of smoke."The sun will be turned into darkness and the moon into blood before the great and awesome day of the Lord comes. And it will come about that whoever calls on the name of the Lord will be saved.

Here is the fulfillment and Peter's statement about this prophecy and his explanation of what was happening and how the apostles were speaking in foreign languages they had never before learned.

Acts 2:1-4; 15-18

When the day of Pentecost had come, they were all together in one place. And suddenly there came from heaven a noise like a violent rushing wind, and it filled the whole house where they were sitting. And there appeared to them tongues as of fire distributing themselves, and they rested on each one of them. And they were all filled with the Holy Spirit and began to speak with other tongues, as the Spirit was giving them utterance.

But Peter, taking his stand <u>with the eleven</u>, raised his voice and declared to them: "Men of Judea and all you who live in Jerusalem let this be known to you and give heed to my words. For these men are not drunk, as you suppose, for it is only the third hour of the day; but this is what was spoken of through the prophet Joel:

'And it shall be in the last days,' God says, 'that I will pour forth of My spirit on all mankind; and your sons and your daughters

shall prophesy, and your young men shall see visions, and your old men shall dream dreams; Even on my bond slaves, both men and women, I will in those days pour forth of My spirit and they shall prophesy. And I will grant wonders in the sky above and signs on the earth below, blood, and fire, and vapor of smoke. The sun will be turned into darkness and the moon into blood, before the great and glorious day of the Lord shall come. And it shall be that everyone who calls on the name of the Lord will be saved.

Prophetic language is often quite dynamic. He uses terms like *Blood and fire and vapor of smoke, the sun will be turned into darkness and the moon into blood.* Those things weren't happening on that day, but the Spirit coming is what Joel was specifically predicting; and it was fulfilled. It was Jesus who sent the Holy Spirit as was also predicted (John 1:33).

The baptism in the Holy Spirit directly empowered men to perform miracles as in the case of the apostles (Acts 2:1-4) and the household of Cornelius (Acts 10:46). This is different than the imparting of the miraculous gifts of the Spirit by the laying on of the apostles hands which we'll examined shortly.

The Baptism in the Holy Spirit is:
1. Not a promise to everyone (Acts 1:8). It was promised to the apostles.
1. Not administered by man (Matthew 3:11). It's administered only by Jesus.
2. Not received by the laying on of hands (Acts 8:17-18). After the apostles were baptized in the Spirit, they could lay hands on other believers and give them individual miraculous gifts.
3. Not conversion or salvation (Acts 10:46-18; 11:15). In the conversion account of Cornelius, they were baptized in the Holy Spirit to prove to Peter and his friends that the Gentiles were also recipients of the Gospel and could not be rejected. After Cornelius' household was baptized in the Holy Spirit, Peter then willingly baptized them in water for the forgiveness of sins and at that time they also received the indwelling of the Spirit.

4. Not inspiration (Acts 10:48; 11:14). The preached message saves.
5. Not water baptism (Matthew 3:11; Acts 10:47-49). Water baptism is commanded and can be obeyed. Baptism in the Holy Spirit was a promise and given directly by Jesus Himself.

Two accounts of Holy Spirit Baptism in Scripture:

The purpose of the Holy Spirit baptism was to mark the beginning of a significant event.

1. Marked the beginning of the church and the first gospel sermon preached to the Jews (Acts 2).
2. Marked the beginning of the Gospel being taken to the Gentiles and demonstrated God's acceptance of them (Read Acts 10 and 11).

Let's discuss the occurrence on Cornelius' household. He was a Gentile and up to this time the Jews assumed that they alone had access to the Gospel of Christ. This was ten years after the church began in Acts 2. Up to this time, no Gentiles other than those who had converted to Judaism had accepted the Gospel of Christ. In fact, it was thought to be a violation of God's law for a Jew to associate or eat with a Gentile; they were thought to be unclean and untouchable.

God coordinated a meeting between Cornelius and Peter by sending an angel who told Peter to have no reservation about visiting and eating with this Gentile. Cornelius welcomes Peter and asks him about the message God had for him and his family. As Peter is preaching, Cornelius' household is baptized in the Holy Spirit. Let's look at the text on how this happened.

Acts10:

Cornelius's Vision

Now there was a man at Caesarea named Cornelius, a centurion of what was called the Italian cohort, a devout man and one who feared God with all his household, and gave many alms to the Jewish people and prayed to God continually. About the ninth hour of the day he clearly saw in a vision an angel of

God who had just come in and said to him, "Cornelius!" And fixing his gaze on him and being much alarmed, he said, "What is it, Lord?" And he said to him, "Your prayers and alms have ascended as a memorial before God. Now dispatch some men to Joppa and send for a man named Simon, who is also called Peter; he is staying with a tanner named Simon, whose house is by the sea."

Meanwhile, in Joppa Peter has a vision. The vision happens three times so that "at the mouth of two or three witnesses every fact shall be established." The message to Peter was that he could no longer consider Gentiles unclean and he was to proceed to Cornelius' home without hesitation.

On the next day, as they were on their way and approaching the city, Peter went up on the housetop about the sixth hour to pray. But he became hungry and was desiring to eat; but while they were making preparations, he fell into a trance; and he saw the sky opened up, and an object like a great sheet coming down, lowered by four corners to the ground, and there were in it all kinds of four-footed animals and crawling creatures of the earth and birds of the air. A voice came to him, "Get up, Peter, kill and eat!" But Peter said, "By no means, Lord, for I have never eaten anything unholy and unclean." Again a voice came to him a second time, "What God has cleansed, no longer consider unholy." This happened three times, and immediately the object was taken up into the sky.

Peter then travels to Caesarea:

*While Peter was reflecting on the vision, the Spirit said to him, "Behold, three men are looking for you. But get up, go downstairs and accompany them without misgivings, for I have sent them Myself." Peter went down to the men and said, "Behold, I am the one you are looking for; what is the reason for which you have come?" They said, "Cornelius, a centurion, a righteous and God-fearing man well spoken of by the entire nation of the Jews, was divinely directed by a holy angel to send for you to come to his house and **hear a message from you**."*

171

Peter at Caesarea

And on the next day he got up and went away with them, and some of the brethren from Joppa accompanied him. On the following day he entered Caesarea. Now Cornelius was waiting for them and had called together his relatives and close friends.

Peter's message and the baptism of the Holy Spirit

Opening his mouth, Peter said:

"I most certainly understand now that God is not one to show partiality,(the vision of the unclean animals) but in every nation the man who fears Him and does what is right is welcome to Him. The word which He sent to the sons of Israel, preaching peace through Jesus Christ (He is Lord of all) you yourselves know the thing which took place throughout all Judea, starting from Galilee, after the baptism which John proclaimed. You know of Jesus of Nazareth, how God anointed Him with the Holy Spirit and with power, and how He went about doing good and healing all who were oppressed by the devil, for God was with Him. We are witnesses of all the things He did both in the land of the Jews and in Jerusalem. They also put Him to death by hanging Him on a cross. God raised Him up on the third day and granted that He become visible, not to all the people, but to witnesses who were chosen beforehand by God, that is, to us who ate and drank with Him after He arose from the dead. And He ordered us to preach to the people, and solemnly to testify that this is the One who has been appointed by God as Judge of the living and the dead. Of Him all the prophets bear witness that through His name everyone who believes in Him receives forgiveness of sins."

While Peter was still speaking these words, the Holy Spirit fell upon all those who were listening to the message. All the circumcised believers who came with Peter were amazed, <u>because the gift of the Holy Spirit had been poured out on the Gentiles also</u>. *For they were hearing them speaking with tongues and exalting God. Then Peter answered, <u>"Surely no one can refuse the water for these to be baptized who have received the</u>*

*Holy Spirit just as we did, can he?" And he ordered them to be
baptized in the name of Jesus Christ. Then they asked him to stay
on for a few days.*

Peter and his companions travel back to Jerusalem and were
reprimanded for going into the house of a Gentile and eating with him.
Peter recounts that they were baptized in the Holy Spirit just as had
occurred to the apostles ten years earlier and that convinced him that
they must accept the Gentiles into the church.

*And when Peter came up to Jerusalem, those who were
circumcised took issue with him, saying, "You went to
uncircumcised men and ate with them," (Acts 11:2-3).*

*And as I began to speak, the Holy Spirit fell upon them **just as He
did upon us at the beginning** (ten years earlier). And I
remembered the word of the Lord, how He used to say, 'John
baptized with water, but you will be baptized with the Holy
Spirit.' Therefore if God gave to them the same gift as He gave to
us also after believing in the Lord Jesus Christ, who was I that I
could stand in God's way?" When they heard this, they quieted
down and glorified God, saying, **"Well then, God has granted to
the Gentiles also the repentance that leads to life,"** (Acts 11:15-
18).*

God demonstrated with a miraculous occurrence the introduction of
both Jews and Gentiles into the kingdom of God. Once "All flesh" was
shown to be acceptable to God, the PURPOSE of Holy Spirit Baptism
ceased. Now, according to Paul, there is only one baptism and as we will
see, that is water baptism in the name of Jesus for forgiveness of sins.

Ephesians 4:4-5

*There is one body and one Spirit, just as also you were called in
one hope of your calling; one Lord, one faith, **one baptism**, one
God and Father of all who is over all and through all and in all.*

Now let's examine that one baptism. In the Bible there were four that
are mentioned- John's baptism; Baptism of the Holy Spirit; Baptism of

Fire (Judgment); and Baptism in the name of Jesus for the forgiveness of sins and to receive the indwelling of the Holy Spirit.

1. John's baptism was no longer valid after the death of Christ (Acts 19:1-5).
2. Baptism of the Holy Spirit occurred only twice;
   a. **On Pentecost, AD 33 upon the apostles only.**
      i. He gives <u>orders</u> **to the apostles** to stay in <u>Jerusalem</u> and <u>commanded THEM not to leave Jerusalem but to wait for what the Father had promised</u>..**YOU (not the 120)** <u>will be baptized with the Holy Spirit not many days from now</u> (Acts 1:2,4).
      ii. *"And they drew lots and the lot fell to Matthias, <u>and he was numbered and added to the eleven apostles"</u>* (Acts 2:26). Note, there is no chapter break in the original so the thought continues.
      iii. *"When the day of Pentecost had come, they (the apostles) were all together in one place. And suddenly there came from heaven a noise like a violent rushing wind, and it filled the whole house where they (the apostles) were sitting. And there appeared to them (the apostles) tongues as of fire distributing themselves, and they rested on each one of them (the apostles). And they (the apostles) were all filled with the Holy Spirit and began to speak with other tongues, as the Spirit was giving them (the apostles) utterance"* (Acts 2:1-4).
      iv. *"They (the crowd) were amazed and astonished, saying, "Why, **<u>are not all these who are speaking Galileans</u>** (the apostles not the 120). And how is it that we each hear them (the apostles) in our own language to which we were born,"* (Acts 2:7)?
      v. *But Peter, taking his stand<u> with the eleven</u> (not the 120), raised his voice and declared to them: "Men of Judea and all you who live in Jerusalem*

*let this be known to you and give heed to my words. For these men (**Males; the apostles**) are not drunk, as you suppose* (Acts 2:14-15).

vi. *"Now when they heard this, they were pierced to the heart, and <u>said to Peter and the rest of the apostles</u>, (not the 120) "Brothers (men, not women)*, what shall we do"* (Acts 2:37).

vii. *"Everyone kept feeling a sense of awe; and many wonders and signs were taking place <u>through the apostles"</u>* (not the 120) (Acts 2: 43).

viii. When one examines the text carefully it's obvious that the baptism of the Holy Spirit and the miracles that accompanied it including the speaking in other languages happened to the apostles only.

b. **The second account of the baptism in the Holy Spirit occurred on Cornelius's household to convince the Jews that the Gentiles could now be allowed into the kingdom of God** (Acts 10-11)

Now let's examine the timeline of events.
- Acts 10-11 is dated AD 43 – two baptisms - water and Holy Spirit.
- By AD 60, Paul said there was only ONE baptism (Ephesians 4:4-5).
- After AD 60 Peter says water baptism is the one baptism still valid (1 Peter 3:21)
- The one baptism, therefore, is water baptism in the name of Jesus for the forgiveness of sins and to receive the promise of the indwelling of the Holy Spirit (Acts 2:38; Matthew 28:19).

IV. Conclusion

The indwelling of the Spirit is a promise given to all who are baptized into Christ. The indwelling Spirit has no miraculous accompaniment but is a wonderful promise of God. The giving of the indwelling Spirit is God's down payment on our redemption. It is His promise that guarantees our inheritance. The Holy Spirit is God's seal upon us showing that we belong to Him and that He is committed to our salvation.

The Baptism of the Holy Spirit occurred only twice in the Bible and marked the beginning of two significant events:
1. The beginning of the church and the first Jewish converts to Christianity.
2. The beginning of the gospel to the Gentiles and the first Gentile converts outside of Judaism.

There is only one valid baptism in the plan of God today, and that is water baptism in the name of Jesus. The purpose of that baptism is to receive the forgiveness of sins and the gift of the indwelling of the Holy Spirit.

Chapter 9 – Miraculous Gifts of the Holy Spirit

Now we must address the miraculous manifestations of the Holy Spirit. There were miraculous gifts given to believers in the early church that included prophecy, speaking fluently in languages you never before studied (tongues) interpretation of tongues; miraculous and instant healing by the laying on of hands, raising the dead; prophecy, and miraculous knowledge.

These gifts were sometimes misused and believers in the Corinthian church were comparing their miraculous gifts and exalting themselves because one gift may be more visible than another. 1 Corinthians 12 is an instruction manual as it were on how not to misuse spiritual gifts. Not everyone had the same miraculous gift and some had none at all, but they were all in Christ and had the indwelling of the Spirit so their comparisons were childish and immature. Everyone is gifted by the Spirit - miraculous or not. In fact, Paul describes the miraculous gifts in this way, *"When I was a child, I used to speak like a child, think like a child, reason like a child; when I became a man, I did away with childish things (1 Corinthians 13:11).*

Paul goes on in Chapter 13 to show that love is the supreme quality of a believer and exhorts them to not get too hung up on miraculous gifts because they are temporary. The things that will last are faith, hope and love. Tongues, miraculous knowledge and prophecy are temporary and will pass away but faith, hope and love will remain and the greatest of these would be love because unlike faith and hope, love will last into eternity. Faith and hope will be swallowed up in sight when Jesus is revealed and we will no longer need to hope for that which we now see.

Let's review what we've learned. From our last chapter, we have seen that there are three measures or manifestations of the Holy Spirit:
1. The indwelling of the Holy Spirit.
2. The Baptism of the Holy Spirit.
3. The miraculous gifts of the Spirit.

We learned that the indwelling of the Spirit is for all who are obedient to the Lord and become Christians. The indwelling is given at the point of baptism (Acts 2:38; Ephesians 1:13-14; John 3:3-5).

We have also seen that the Baptism of the Holy Spirit occurred only twice (Acts 2 and Acts 10). Both occurrences introduced the Gospel to a particular group of people:
1. The beginning of the gospel introduction to the Jews (Acts 2).
2. The beginning of the gospel introduction to the Gentiles (Acts 10).

We have also demonstrated that by the time that Ephesians was written, there was only one valid baptism in effect at that time (Ephesians 4:4-5). That one baptism was water baptism in the name of Jesus in order to receive the forgiveness of sins (Acts 22:16; 1 Peter 3:21). In this chapter we will examine the miraculous manifestations of the Spirit.

I. The purpose of miracles
God did miracles through several people in the Old Testament. The Jews were in bondage in Egypt and God sent Moses to Pharaoh with a message. When God told Moses to preach to Pharaoh he gave Moses the ability to do miraculous signs to prove that this was in fact a message from God.

Exodus 4:1-8; 29-30

Then Moses said, "What if they will not believe me or listen to what I say? For they may say, 'The Lord has not appeared to you.'" The Lord said to him, "What is that in your hand?" And he said, "A staff." Then He said, "Throw it on the ground." So he threw it on the ground, and it became a serpent; and Moses fled

178

from it. But the Lord said to Moses, "Stretch out your hand and grasp it by its tail"-so he stretched out his hand and caught it, and it became a staff in his hand- "**that they may believe that the Lord, the God of their fathers, the God of Abraham, the God of Isaac, and the God of Jacob, has appeared to you.**"

The Lord furthermore said to him, "Now put your hand into your bosom." So he put his hand into his bosom, and when he took it out, behold, his hand was leprous like snow. Then He said, "Put your hand into your bosom again." So he put his hand into his bosom again, and when he took it out of his bosom, behold, it was restored like the rest of his flesh. "If they will not believe you or heed the witness of the first sign, they may believe the witness of the last sign. But if they will not believe even these two signs or heed what you say, then you shall take some water from the Nile and pour it on the dry ground; and the water which you take from the Nile will become blood on the dry ground."(Exodus 4:1-9).

Exodus 4:29-30

Moses told Aaron all the words of the Lord with which He had sent him and all the signs that He had commanded him to do. Then Moses and Aaron went and assembled all the elders of the sons of Israel; and Aaron spoke all the words which the Lord had spoken to Moses**. He then performed the signs in the sight of the people. So the people believed; and when they heard** that the Lord was concerned about the sons of Israel and that He had seen their affliction, and then they bowed low and worshiped.

Moses spoke the truth and then confirmed it with miracles and the people believed. There was no written scripture at this time. Moses couldn't point to book, chapter and verse to show what God wanted. So before there was a written word, God used miracles to confirm His message spoken through the prophet.

Jesus also performed miracles to confirm His mission to the world. He did many other miracles than those we have record of, but the ones that He did do were recorded and written in scripture. When we read the account of those miracles the Holy Spirit produces faith in good hearts and we believe and ultimately have life in His name as a result. Let's take a look at some examples from scripture.

John 20:30-31

> *Therefore many other signs Jesus also performed in the presence of the disciples which are not written in this book; but these have been written so that you may believe that Jesus is the Christ, the Son of God; and that believing you may have life in His name.*

John 10:37-38

> *If I do not do the works of My Father, do not believe Me; but if I do them, though you do not believe Me, believe the works (signs), so that you may know and understand that the Father is in Me, and I in the Father."*

The miracles that Jesus performed were recorded in Scripture by inspiration of the Holy Spirit. Faith comes by hearing the Word of God (Romans 1:17); therefore when we read these miraculous accounts it produces faith in the heart of those who read and understand. Notice the sequence – Jesus spoke the message. He confirmed the message with miracles. The miracles were then written down. When we read the written scripture, those miracles produce faith in us as we read and hear.

Are you seeing the pattern here? A prophet, apostle or Jesus spoke a message from God before there was confirmed scripture. God had to establish the credibility of the message as being authentic and from Him; so He intervened with a miraculous sign or wonder to in effect "Notarize" the message as being legitimate.

Jesus sent the apostles into the world to preach the Gospel, but after His ascension why should anyone believe them? Jesus continued to work with them to authenticate the message He commissioned them to preach.

> *Mark 16:20*
>
> *So then, when the Lord Jesus had spoken to them, He was received up into heaven and sat down at the right hand of God. And they went out and preached everywhere, while **the Lord worked with them, and confirmed the word by the signs that followed.***

Throughout the establishment of the New Covenant and expanse of the Gospel, miracles were used to confirm the spoken message as being authentic until written scripture was established. The word was first spoken; then it was confirmed by miracles; then ultimately written down. When we read that which is written, it produces faith just as if we had seen the miracle personally.

> *Hebrews 2:2-4*
>
> *For if the word spoken through angels proved unalterable, and every transgression and disobedience received a just penalty, how will we escape if we neglect so great a salvation? <u>After it was at the first spoken</u> through the Lord, <u>it was confirmed</u> to us by those who heard, <u>God also testifying with them, both by signs and wonders and by various miracles and by gifts of the Holy Spirit according to His own will</u>.*

The word "confirmed" means: "to make firm, establish, make sure," (W.E. Vine, Expository Dictionary of New Testament Words). The gospel that was preached was a new message to the world as was the Ten Commandments to Israel. Miracles were used to accompany the spoken word in order to confirm its authority as the word of God. Once written, the written scripture became authoritative and was capable of producing saving faith (John 20:30-31).

Once something is confirmed or established, it no longer needs to be reconfirmed over and over again. Once a document is notarized, you don't have to notarize it every time you look at it. Once authenticated, it's authentic forever by the authority of the Notary. The Notary is an official authorized by the State to verify the authenticity of documents and signatures. Miracles were the Notary that authenticated the message from God and then it was written down and is just as authentic as when first spoken and then written. The scripture is true today because it has already been confirmed and Notarized by God Himself and doesn't need to be reconfirmed any longer.

II. How were miracles imparted?

Miracles were imparted directly from God to certain people in the Old Testament; but in the New Testament God directly imparted miracles only two times other than Jesus Himself. He empowered the apostles and the household of Cornelius to speak in other languages when they were baptized by the Holy Spirit which we've already shown occurred only two times (Acts 2 and Acts 10). There is only one valid baptism today so miracles imparted in this manner are no longer available and we have no record of it occurring in any of the churches throughout the New Testament. Certainly an event of such magnitude would be spoken about frequently had it occurred regularly.

Let's take a close examination of how miracles were given to others as we progress past Pentecost. To do so we have to travel to Samaria. A severe persecution occurred in Jerusalem that scattered the believers to Judea and Samaria. Phillip, one of the first evangelists, travelled to Samaria and proclaimed Christ to them and they not only heard, but they observed the signs that he performed.

> *Acts 8:4-7*
>
> *For in the case of many who had unclean spirits, they were coming out of them shouting with a loud voice; and many who had been paralyzed and lame were healed. So there was much rejoicing in that city.*

There was a magician in the city named Simon who formerly practiced magic that astonished the people and he claimed that he was someone great and everybody in town gave him accolades claiming that he is "The Great Power of God." For a long time he had astonished them with his magic arts (Acts 8:10-11). I'm sure you've seen incredible magicians.

I still can't figure out some of the things I've seen on TV or when visiting Vegas. How can you cut someone in half and have their head on a table three feet away? Don't know, but I know it's an illusion and not a miracle. Some magicians are very skilled in their delusions; but they aren't' miracles from God or even close.

Now I want you to notice Simon's response to Phillip's miracles. He knew that his magic didn't compare to what he saw Phillip doing.

Acts 8:12-13

But when they believed Philip preaching the good news about the kingdom of God and the name of Jesus Christ, they were being baptized, men and women alike. Even Simon himself believed; and after being baptized, he continued on with Philip, and as <u>he observed signs and great miracles taking place, he was constantly amazed.</u>

Philip the evangelist could perform miracles because the apostles had laid their hands on him (Acts 6:5-6). Philip, however, could not impart the gifts to others. It required the apostles (Peter and John) to impart the miraculous gifts to others by the laying on of their hands. This is what Simon observed and he wanted to purchase the ability to pass on miracles like the apostles could. If he could have this power he could make a lot of money.

Acts 8:17-19

Then they (the apostles Peter and John) began laying their hands on them, and they were receiving the (miraculous gifts of the Holy Spirit). <u>Now when Simon saw that the Spirit was bestowed through the laying on of the apostles' hands,</u> he offered them money, saying, "Give this authority to me as well, so that everyone on whom I lay my hands may receive the Holy Spirit."

Now here's a question: since people in the New Testament times could not receive the miraculous gifts of the Holy Spirit without the laying on of the apostle's hands, how can people today? If Philip couldn't pass on miraculous gifts to others; how can people claim to have them today? I don't think they can; and whatever one might claim are legitimate miracles today are counterfeit. They might look like the real thing to the untrained eye; but when compared with scripture; they fail the test.

The gift of tongues was a miraculous ability to speak fluently in a foreign language that was not studied or learned. We see this in Acts 2:6-8, *"And when this sound occurred, the crowd came together, and were bewildered because each one of them was hearing them speak in his own language. They were amazed and astonished, saying, "Why, are not all these who are speaking Galileans? And how is it that we each hear them in our own language to which we were born?* Each of the apostles was speaking a different language and I can imagine that different groups were huddled near the apostle who was speaking their native language. As they would be listening, the other apostles would be speaking a language they did not understand and it might have sounded confusing; but I think you get the point.

Every missionary today that is sent abroad to a foreign country must first take classes to learn the language. If people had the legitimate gift of tongues today this would be unnecessary. Now if you had the gift of tongues and let's say you could speak Romanian miraculously; then I might not understand you, so someone would have to have the gift of interpretation to tell me what you are saying. However a Romanian would be able to understand you and would be amazed that you could speak his language fluently. This was the gift of tongues and it's not what you see people doing today who claim to speak in tongues.

III. Duration of miraculous gifts
Miraculous gifts were present in the early church; no one can deny that. We've seen from the Samaritan account in Acts 8 that miracles were imparted to other believers by the laying on of the apostle's hands.

Believers in the infant church misused these gifts and often compared themselves with others with less visible gifts; thinking that their gift (like speaking in tongues) was superior to others who might have a less visible gift such as miraculous knowledge. Paul addressed this error in his letter to the Corinthians and reminds these believers that these miraculous gifts were temporary and childish when compared to the

184

actions of those who are mature. He reminds them that miraculous gifts of prophecy would be done away, miraculous tongues would cease, and miraculous knowledge would be done away. These were *parts* or pieces of something that later would be complete. These were what a child needed until he was mature; then once mature he would put away these childish things.

1 Corinthians 13:8-13

Love never fails; but if there are <u>gifts of prophecy, they will be done away; if there are tongues, they will cease; if there is knowledge, it will be done away</u>. For we know in part and we prophecy in part; but when the perfect (thing) comes; the partial (things) will be done away. When I was a child, I used to speak like a child, think like a child, reason like a child; when I became a man, I did away with childish things... But now faith, hope, love, abide these three; but the greatest of these is love.

Please note some important statements from this section of scripture:

1. It claims that the miraculous gift of prophecy would be done away.
2. It claims that the miraculous gift of tongues would cease.
3. It claims that the miraculous gift of knowledge would be done away.
4. These miraculous gifts would be done away and cease while faith, hope and love would continue.

It's important to see the contrast between the temporary miraculous gifts and the more permanent aspect of faith, hope and love. We will see in just a few minutes that faith and hope are also temporary and will be swallowed up in sight when Jesus is revealed. So the miraculous gifts would cease well before Jesus' return when *that <u>thing</u> which is perfect* has come.

In the Greek, a generic noun is used to describe tongues, knowledge and prophecy as partial *things* and is contrasted with something that is also a generic *perfect THING. The l*iteral Greek rendering says, *"For in*

185

part we know, and in part we prophecy, <u>but when comes the perfect thing, the things in part will be abolished."</u>

Please notice that this is referring to a *thing* and not a person; when the perfect "thing" comes (not the perfect one). "Thing" is a neuter gender noun in the Greek, therefore the "perfect thing" is not Christ. Christ is not a "thing".

The word, "Perfect"(telios) "signifies having reached its end, finished or complete" (W.E. Vine, Expository Dictionary of New Testament Words). In verse 9, Paul names the partial things (partial knowledge, partial prophecy). The perfect, completed, finished, mature product would be the completed revelation of knowledge and prophecy. The "perfect thing" has to be the completion or end result of the "partial things", therefore the perfect thing must be of the same nature and same kind. This would be similar to saying, "for we have part which is a scaffold, and part which is a bridge crane, but when the completed perfect bridge is erected, the partial things will no longer be needed."

Miracles were used by God to confirm the spoken word before there was a complete written Bible. How could people know for certain that Moses or the apostles were speaking a legitimate word from God unless He confirmed their message with undeniable miraculous confirmation?

> *Hebrews 2:2-4*
>
> *For if the word spoken through angels proved unalterable; how will we escape if we neglect so great a salvation? After it was first SPOKEN through the Lord, it was CONFIRMED to us by those who heard, God also testifying with them, BOTH BY SIGNS AND WONDERS AND BY VARIOUS MIRACLES AND BI GIFTS OF THE HOLY SPIRIT according to his own will.*

When the apostles and prophets in the New Testament spoke and wrote they were revealing parts of God's revelation a bit at a time. Once the perfect revelation was fully revealed, the completion of those parts was finished. Partial knowledge and partial prophecy was now perfect. When the perfect thing was finished the partial things were done away and no longer needed. That which had become mature put away childish things – tongues, partial knowledge and partial prophecy.

2 Timothy 3:16-17

All Scripture is inspired by God and profitable for teaching, for reproof, for correction, for training in righteousness; so that the man of God may be adequate, equipped for every good work.

The written scripture is all we need to be equipped for every good work. It's profitable for teaching, reproof, correction and training in righteousness. James calls the scripture the "PERFECT law of liberty." Now that we have the completed New Testament record there is no longer any need for miraculous confirmation.

Let's examine the time line for when the partial things would be done away. Remember, they are temporary when compared to faith and hope. "Faith is the assurance of things hoped for, the evidence of things not seen," (Hebrews 11:1). So when we see Jesus, we will no longer need faith because we will see Him. Paul explains that we will not have to hope once we see the reality of our salvation. "For in hope we have been saved, but hope that is seen is not hope; for who hopes for what he already sees," (Romans 8:24)?

Therefore, the partial gifts of knowledge, prophecy, and tongues were to cease **before** the second coming of Jesus. They were to cease when the "perfect thing" came. The perfect thing has to be the end result or mature product of tongues, prophecy, and knowledge Tongues, prophecy, and knowledge were for revealing parts and confirming the message of God to man, therefore when the message was completed, the miracles had accomplished their purpose. The perfect, mature thing was complete and the partial things could now be done away.

IV. Conclusion

Miracles were for the purpose of confirming the spoken word of God as being true and from God. Once the word was confirmed and written, the purpose of miracles ceased (John 20:30-31; 2 Timothy 3:15-17).

With the dying of the last apostle, the ability to impart miraculous power to others ceased. With the last letter of the apostles written the perfect, completed word of God had been given and confirmed as being true and from God. Therefore, the partial things ceased with the completion of the revelation of the New Testament books.

Those who claim to have the gifts of prophecy cannot agree even among themselves as to their teaching. Note all the different churches that claim to have the same spirit of prophecy (Mormons, Pentecostals, Catholics, Christian Science, Oral Roberts and his vision of an 800 foot Jesus, as well as many satanic cults and mystery religions; just to name a few). Those who practice voodoo as well as other cultic practices also speak in some unknown tongue; but rest assured that is not of God! God is not the author of confusion; but these teachings all contradict one another and they definitely contradict the Bible and the revealed plan of salvation. Therefore, their message and practice is not from God. And the miracles they claim to perform are false and deceptive tools of Satan. *"For false Christs and false prophets will arise, and will show signs and wonders in order to lead astray, if possible, the elect,"* (Mark 14:22).

Satan's character is to deceive with counterfeit signs and wonders in order to deceive and lead people astray. If people are gullible enough to ignore plain teaching in Scripture, God will send them a strong delusion to help them believe the lie. *"The coming of the lawless one will be in accordance with how Satan works. He will use all sorts of displays of power through signs and wonders that serve the lie, and all the ways that wickedness deceives those who are perishing. They perish because they refused to love the truth and so be saved. For this reason God sends them a powerful delusion so that they will believe the lie* and so that all will be condemned who have not believed the truth but have delighted in wickedness,"* (2 Thessalonians 2:9-12).

In the Old Testament, Moses warned about false prophets who performed signs, wonders and actually made predictions that came true. So how do you "Test" the legitimacy of such miracles? Moses said you test the miracles against the scripture and if the teaching of the prophet doesn't match; you can be assured its false. God is giving a test to see if you follow a sign or wonder or follow the Lord's teaching.

Deuteronomy 13:1-3

*"If a prophet or a dreamer of dreams arises among you and gives you a sign or a wonder, **and the sign or the wonder comes true,** concerning which he spoke to you, saying, 'Let us go after other gods (whom you have not known) and let us serve them,' you shall not listen to the words of that prophet or that dreamer of dreams; for the Lord your God is testing you to find out if you love the Lord your God with all your heart and with all your soul.*

People claim to do miracles; but I want you to remember a verse we looked at previously.

Matthew 7:21-23

"Not everyone who says to Me, 'Lord, Lord,' will enter the kingdom of heaven, but he who does the will of My Father who is in heaven will enter. Many will say to Me on that day, 'Lord, Lord, did we not prophesy in Your name, and in Your name cast out demons, and in Your name perform many miracles?' And then I will declare to them, 'I never knew you; depart from me, you who practice lawlessness.'

Miraculous gifts of the Holy Spirit have ceased. God does still give the indwelling of the Holy Spirit to those who have been baptized into Christ for the forgiveness of sins as a seal of their inheritance (Ephesians 1:13-14; 4:30; Acts 2:38).

God is still active in the world

To say that the temporary miraculous manifestations have ceased in no way suggests that God is not very active in the lives of believers. For instance, James instructs the church about praying to God in order to be healed. *"Is anyone among you sick? Let them call the elders of the church to pray over them and anoint them with oil in the name of the Lord. And the prayer offered in faith will make the sick person well; the*

Lord will raise them up. If they have sinned, they will be forgiven," (James 5:14-15).

We had a good friend at church that was diagnosed with a life-threatening brain tumor. We began praying and fasting that God would heal him. On the day of his scheduled surgery he requested another MRI. The doctor reminded him that he'd already had twelve of them, but reluctantly agreed. The tests revealed that the tumor was completely gone. I've seen God work like this many times and in many ways. I share this just to assure you that God is still fully engaged even though the temporary miraculous gifts of the Spirit that were for revealing and confirming the Bible are no longer needed.

Some final words
I hope this book has given you an introduction to Building Your Relationship with God. You've learned some background about the Bible and that it is the most sought after piece of literature in human history; and for good reason – it is God's love letter that gives us eternal life. You've seen the claims about Jesus and the evidence for His resurrection. You then learned how the Bible was revealed and why we are now under a New Covenant. You've seen the requirements to become a disciple of Jesus and the Biblical plan of salvation.

We explored the New Testament church and seen that the kingdom of God is here. You've learned about the Holy Spirit and the miraculous gifts that were used to reveal the word of God.

If this information is new to you; you might want to re-read it and take notes. You can find more of my study guides that are free of charge at www.gregbiblestudy.blogspot.com. Feel free to share this resource.

May God richly bless your personal walk with God as you grow in grace and knowledge of our Lord and Savior Jesus Christ. To Him be all glory and praise.

Greg King
October 19, 2018

68653251R00111

Made in the USA
Columbia, SC
09 August 2019